THE LANDSCAPE OF HOME

THE LANDSCAPE OF HOME

IN THE COUNTRY, BY THE SEA, IN THE CITY

HOLLANDER DESIGN
LANDSCAPE ARCHITECTS

FOREWORD BY BUNNY WILLIAMS
WRITTEN WITH JUDITH NASATIR

RIZZOLI
NEW YORK

New York Paris London Milan

With humility, we dedicate this book to our clients.
You entrust us to create beautiful, healthy landscapes
for your homes and families—and we are grateful.

Contents

FOREWORD

What is it that makes Ed Hollander and his team one of the top landscape design firms in the country? It is their respect of the site, understanding of the architecture, and bold and exciting use of plant material. I have been lucky to work with Ed on several projects, and walking around a site with him is a marvel. Telling a client that their existing driveway was in the wrong place was not what they wanted to hear, but how right he was, and the new approach made all the difference to the house and property. I walked with him over and over a difficult site for a new home with the architect and clients figuring out where to position the house, the pool, and the accessory building. Specimen trees were marked to be saved, which made the planning even more difficult, but then Ed has such respect for existing mature plantings. All this was done before a pen was put to paper.

Ed starts with the style of architecture, and studies the interior floor plans to focus on views and access points. He has discussions on how the clients envision living on the outside to allow for terraces for alfresco dining, a lawn for children to play, or a location for future tents for a grand party.

Because Ed loves and encourages collaborative work, there is always a perfect relationship between the interior and the exterior. His choices of hard surfaces are always sensitive to the materials used on the house, and the details of the landscape design are always totally compatible with the architecture. Ed paints with the palette of the plants and sculpts with the forms of trees and shrubs. Whether it is a meadow with mown paths or a formal parterre, the gardens he creates seem in total harmony with the house and the land.

Personally, I can also say Ed Hollander is one of the most generous and caring men I know. Whenever asked for a donation for a charity, he says "yes" with a wide-open heart, and his commitment to sharing his talent with others will be a source of inspiration for years to come.
—Bunny Williams

INTRODUCTION

The landscape of home is joy and delight translated into physical reality, for home is as much a feeling as it is a physical presence. We are in the business of creating places for families to live, love, enjoy, take comfort, and grow old with their children and grandchildren. The only way we know how to do this is to think about the landscape of home holistically, to conceptualize it collaboratively with our clients, their architects, and their interior designers so that the landscape feels as if it grows directly out of the architecture and the site. The more seamless the interaction between interior and exterior living spaces, the more the grounds and the house feel like two hands attached to one head, as if sprung from the same creative source, the more welcoming the landscape of home will be, and the greater its gifts of well-being, refuge, and comfort.

Whether it's two acres at the beach, one hundred acres in the country, or ten thousand square feet on an urban rooftop, each property is in its way a canvas. And every canvas is different. One might incorporate hills, mountains, and streams. Another might feature great trees or fabulous views. And still another might be a flat field primed for sculpting. As we begin to determine what components go into that landscape—the main house and guest house, outdoor rooms for living and lounging, recreational areas, gardens, natural areas, a swimming pool, places for young children, a tennis court, dining terraces, and so on—we think deeply about their placement. How will the spaces and places come together and relate to one another and the overall property? How will the rooms flow from inside to outside, from the living room to a screened porch, covered terrace, or a pergola in the garden, from the dining room to a table sheltered under a magnificent old linden tree? The gracefulness and elegance of those transitions, and the ones that pull us farther afield on the property, give each landscape of home its special feel. Walls and doors can obscure the connection between inside and outside, while spaces that feel ambiguously in between—a porch, a veranda, a covered area open to the elements—can invite and give the sense that the entire property is home.

For us, the starting point of each design is the information the site itself offers from a neighborhood, community, and ecological perspective. We work with the architects to determine how and where the building(s) will sit on the property and engage with the landscape, as well as how each structure is meant to function. We go through a similar information-gathering process with the homeowner to understand their needs and desires; together, we also look at an array of images to begin to develop an idea of what will make this specific house on this unique piece of property the home of their dreams.

Very few landscapes are untouched by man, especially in the United States, and particularly on the East Coast. Our task as landscape architects is not simply to understand and respond to what nature has created. We also need to have a firm grasp on what man has done to the specific piece of property over time; if it's post-agricultural land, for example, how it was farmed and the state of the soils as a result. This combined history of man and nature is where we always begin, and it filters into all our design decision-making. A landscape, after all, is a living thing, the result of all these processes over time. The trees and other existing vegetation, soils, geology, hydrology, light, birds, and wildlife tell us so much about the identity of each place, what is right for it, and how it may change from hour to hour, day to day, and season to season.

Our approach grows out of an ecological model first developed by Ian McHarg, the great landscape architect who was the long-time chair of landscape and regional planning at the University of Pennsylvania, and one of my guiding spirits. Truly larger than life, McHarg was the first to see the planet

as a living, breathing organism, and its elements—including geology, hydrology, soils, vegetation—as part of a complex ecological web.

From the time my partner Maryanne Connelly and I opened our doors on Lafayette Street in 1991 with my mother at the front desk, it's been a family operation defined by an approach, rather than a particular style. This continues to be true with Melissa Reavis, Stephen Eich, and Geoffrey Valentino, my new partners, and at our present size of forty people. We listen to the land, to the architecture, and to the people, and we respond.

We refer to this as the three ecologies: the natural ecology, the architectural ecology, and the human ecology. These are our fundamental starting points. And because no two projects share the same combination, every home is different, which is why there is such a variety of designs in the following pages.

How do we listen to the land? In a multisensory way, observing and absorbing the landscape with as many of our senses as possible. The alchemy of sights, smells, sounds, textures, colors, and movement prompts how we respond. To grasp the nature of the site and what makes it special, wherever it is—in the country, by the sea, or in the city—we need to understand its environment, its ecosystems, and its views.

In a way, landscape architects are both choreographers and composers. We choreograph the positioning and to some extent the movement of plant life and trees, but especially the way that people move into and through a property. And we compose the way a landscape looks and changes through the seasons, because landscapes are never static, ever. Landscapes are constantly evolving: every two weeks new blooms are coming and others receding. The trees, shrubs, flowers, and grasses that make up the planting designs are almost symphonic. Their music crescendos and decrescendos from April through October and ends in a great flourish in November and into December, before it goes quiet. Through the winter, there's the peace of topography and structure and, in the northern climates, snow until April when everything starts to come back to life.

Just as important is the need, really the imperative, to create a healthy landscape for the people and plantings it sustains. We understand that soil is a living thing, so we protect it, cherish it, and, when necessary, work to create it. Healthy soils produce healthy plants. The knowledge of what wants to grow where allows us to shape landscapes and properties that are in tune with nature, and that permit totally organic care whenever possible.

There is a poetry to placement, which is why collaboration is so critical, and why the best-case scenario is when the members of the team—architect, landscape architect, and interior designer—work together from the start. The architecture is always the dominant built form on each property, so the first decisions inevitably involve the procession of entry and the siting of the main house, guest house, and the pool, which is so often a key to all the other elements of the landscape. As we get further into the process, we continue to synthesize ideas from the growing field of people involved, including the builders and even the stonemasons when construction is underway.

As we develop each landscape, we think about the choreography of movement through it and the importance of invitation and orientation, design features stressed by the great landscape architect Ed Bye when I was in graduate school at Penn. We think about that alchemy of the senses. How will the landscape feel? What fragrances will waft in the breezes? What will the soundscape be like as the wind blows through leaves and grasses, the honeybees make their rounds, and the birds burst into song? What colors will delight the eyes, and what plants will attract the butterflies? Can we incorporate orchards of peach trees and apple trees so the homeowners can pick and eat fruit fresh off the tree, which is supremely magical? This doesn't mean that every place on a property needs to be a cacophony of sensual delight. Just that each place should have its own identity: of peace and tranquility; of movement and enclosure; of space to run and to play; of fragrance, color, texture, and sound. The way the various areas of the property delight the senses creates the special landscape of home.

We assist nature, we don't create nature. Yes, we're shaping an environment. And it is so much fun to build: to move mountains of earth, bring in trees, develop pathways. But we always work within nature's parameters, one of which is time. And time is truly essential. It takes skill, experience, and compulsive organization to create a landscape that looks lush and beautiful on move-in day. Yet it will still take time before that landscape manifests itself fully because all plants, even the largest, need time to grow roots, dig into their setting, to make it home.

Home means different things to different people. For us, home is the landscape that people live in, not just look at: that place of refuge, safety, and, most importantly, joy, where family and friends gather to create a lifetime of memories. It is fantastic—and a great privilege—to create this kind of living, changing beauty. But the sheer delight we get from collaborating to create the landscape of home is also a gift. This level of joy permeates everything we do, especially when we see it in the smiles of the families who live in the landscape of home we've created together.

HOME IN THE COUNTRY

The country—pastoral, bucolic, wooded, often agricultural—opens its arms in welcome. With rivers, fields, hills, mountains, lakes, and ponds, it offers a more expansive range of habitats than the oceanfront or the city. This means we can design landscapes as diverse as the properties themselves, and as much as the surrounding environment and the homeowner will allow. We respond to what nature gives us, of course. And we obviously tie each landscape we design to the specific site conditions, region, and family. But because country environments are innately more malleable, they allow us to manipulate the land as we find it in ways that we can't necessarily achieve on the coast and can't even contemplate in the city.

The idea of a country home connotes a host of meanings as diverse as people's histories, backgrounds, and dreams, but it is always an oasis, an escape, and typically a haven for weekends, holidays, and summer months. Some country houses are farms. Others are grander in scope and more formal in style. Still others are in villages. Whether their home lives on an acre, five acres, or a hundred acres, our clients want places where they can gather outside in the sun or shade and see and smell the flowers. Many include a swimming pool, because we are always drawn to water. Most prioritize places for the family to gather, cook, dine, and entertain. Our challenge is to create inviting areas outdoors that work architecturally and fit naturally into the overall flow of living spaces.

The natural ecology is inevitably where we begin. We factor into our conceptual design the ecology of the specific property and the surrounding landscape. Because we work with such a diverse group of architects, we then take into account the architectural ecology of the buildings, which can range from historic and traditional to modern and abstract. What is key for us always is that the integration of landscape and architecture feels seamless. Into that, we combine the human ecology of the individual family and their dreams of how they plan to occupy the space. In other words, we're trying to create a perfect three-way marriage.

When we understand the land as a layer cake of geology, hydrology, soils, and vegetation, we have a paradigm for seeing the surface as a reflection of the dynamic processes that shaped it and can start to envision the land as a living thing. In this way, whether vast or small, each country landscape that we create becomes part of the ongoing, evolving communal story, and of the ecological quilt of the area and its wider surroundings.

OPPOSITE: Country landscapes offer vast possibilities for design, plant, and color palettes. Here, white flowering crape myrtles underplanted with various low ornamental grasses from the Pennisetum and Schizachyrium families and a mix of flowering bulbs and perennials, including Echinacea purpurea and Allium Globemaster, embrace a greensward within a relaxed, native-looking frame.

TOPPING FARM

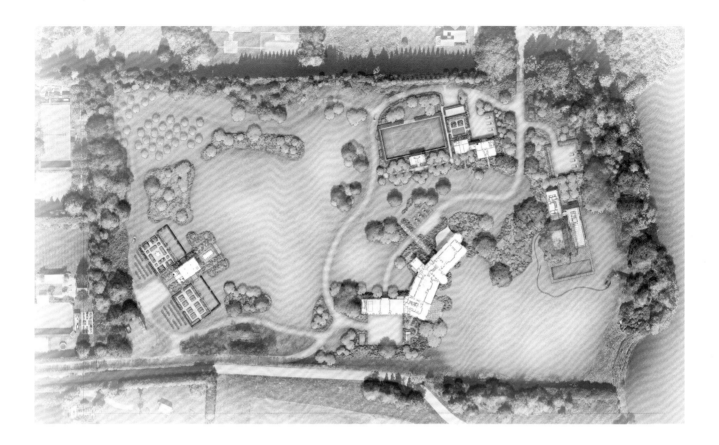

It's rare to come across a fifteen-acre, post-agricultural property that still has much of its long history on display. But here, on this site, the centuries existed right before our eyes. There was a house from the 1700s, wonderfully preserved though needing work, as well as a modest, multistory ranch building from the 1950s. There were fields and farm structures, including dilapidated old barns, the largest birdbath I've ever seen, and an abandoned peacock house. The homeowners, a young family, wanted to incorporate all these traces of the past along with a new main house and pool house/pool area into a home for their future.

They assembled a design team as varied as their three-lot property with its surprising but magnificent centuries-old maple and plane trees, pond frontage, and distant horizon of dune and ocean views. Our collaborators included architect Peter Pennoyer and interior designer Victoria Hagan for the main house; designer Robert Stilin, who renovated the historic structures; and architect Roger Ferris, responsible for the pool house. Our role was to create a landscape that melded together the disparate buildings, fields, pool, tennis court, meadows, working gardens, orchards, and even a renovated chicken coop into a unified home—and made it look as if everything had always been there.

PRECEDING SPREAD: The entry's combination of Connecticut fieldstone posts, traditional farm gate, and blackened steel edging ties together the property's past and present. ABOVE: A key planning feature involved framing site lines and views. OPPOSITE TOP: Blushing Bride hydrangea hedges create a scrim between the gravel drive and the front of the new main house. OPPOSITE: Boxwood clouds border the reclaimed Yorkstone pavers leading to the front door.

PAGES 20 - 21: Existing stands of old-growth trees and water vistas informed the placement of the property's structures and the sinuous curves of its driveways. PRECEDING SPREAD: A crape myrtle allée underplanted with geranium Rozanne and astilbe creates a draw to the guest area and connects it to the agricultural area beyond. RIGHT: A consistent landscape of gravel, grasses, stone walls, shaped evergreen shrubs, and mature trees creates a natural frame for the pool house, a distinctively modern twist on a barn vernacular.

As we sited the buildings, we began thinking about the associated landscape elements, their various relationships, and what could be seen from where. As we gradually removed the accumulated debris of the centuries—preserving the best of what was there and transplanting trees as necessary—the property revealed its bones. These guided our decisions about the entry progression and the most poetic placement of trees to heighten discovery, frame farther vistas, and shape closer views from structure to structure.

The most prominent parcel went rightfully to the main house with its expansive veranda that unfolded to open terraces, a firepit, and a sweeping panorama over the lawn and across the pond. For paving materials, we eventually settled on a reclaimed Yorkstone, quarried in Yorkshire since the Middle Ages, that placed the veracity of history underfoot. We also put up many samples of stone walls and terraces; because we envisioned them ultimately as the thread tying the buildings, and the entire property, together, we wanted to make sure they worked together, and with the

ABOVE: An existing pair of ancient plane trees determined the siting of the guest house and its pool and spa, which unfold seamlessly from the house and reflect its simple forms, glass expanses, and verdant surroundings. OPPOSITE: The sinuous Corten steel picket fence provides a necessary safety barrier for the pool without blocking views across the property.

architecture and other materials, not just in the studio but outside in the site's particular light and conditions. We tried any number of safety barriers for the pool area, veiled from the main house by a grove of trees, and decided on a sinuous, sculptural Corten steel picket fence that allowed total porosity of views.

The couple also wanted a healthy environment where the kids could play. Right next to the tennis court (draped in white wisteria, magically fragrant when it blooms), we created an adventure land with a multilevel village of repurposed tree houses. This led to a large open pasture meadow, perfect for games and running around.

With an organic vegetable garden; cutting gardens; blackberry, raspberry, and blueberry patches; and an orchard of peach, apple, and pear trees—plus a chicken coop made from the old peacock house—the property yields its abundance through the seasons. The landscape has become more than a place for the family and their friends. True to its roots, it remains, as it was through the centuries, a habitat for bees, birds, and butterflies, and all our other friends in the environment.

RIGHT: Espaliered pear trees and bee-friendly lavender grow along the cedar Belgian fence and the archway that marks the entry to the agricultural preserve beyond. Joe-Pye weed, oxeye daisies, sunflowers, black-eyed Susans, and lobelia stud the agricultural preserve's meadow. Two hives tucked into this area allow the bees to feast on flowering peach, pear, and apple orchards.

TOP, LEFT TO RIGHT: The original eighteenth-century farmhouse, repurposed as the guest house. Artful planting screens unwanted views along the edge of the guest house. White wisteria transforms the tennis cabana into a part of the garden. Corten pickets create a see-through fence around the pool. ABOVE, LEFT TO RIGHT: Repurposed Yorkstone paves a yoga area outside the gym. The path from the tennis cabana to the agricultural preserve. Reclaimed granite cobbles and grass carpet the parking area. Wildlife loves this landscape, too.

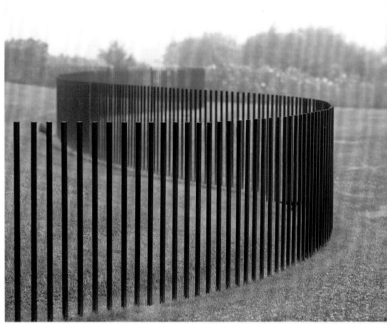

MEADOW FARM

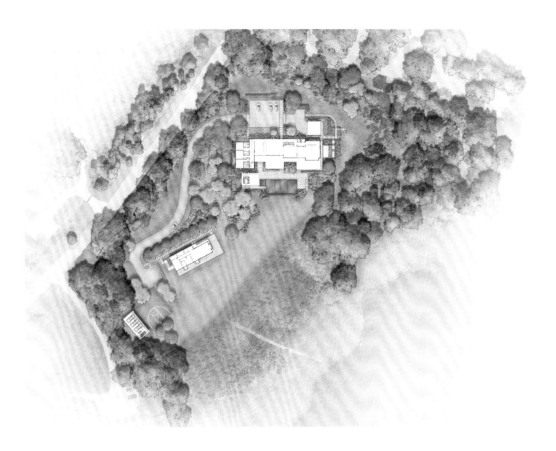

Good design lives on so many levels. Our aim, always, is to cultivate a landscape of home that creates magic, mystery, and delight. Clarity, though, is just as important. Comfort comes when the features of the landscape—entry, driveway, route to the front door, and so on—invite us in and tell us where to go, what to do, and how to do it.

When we began working on this five-acre property with architects Stelle Lomont Rouhani and interior designer Damon Liss, it was raw land and completely flat. The owners had a desire for something that didn't feel like the typical Hamptons landscape (meaning: no hydrangea). We sculpted the topography into a gentle roll, planted some beautiful meadows between the main house and guest house, and connected the two with paths that weave through mounds of wilder shrubs, flowers, and trees to create journeys of joy. Everything we created here—main house, guest house, pool area, terraces, covered and open living and dining spaces, driveway, pathways, meadows, gardens—celebrates the myriad pleasures of life lived out of doors.

All the forms, textures, materials, and plantings reflect and speak directly to the linear modernity of the architecture. At the front of the house, the gravel driveway leads to pavers set first in grass, then in concrete, then as raised steps that create an invitation to the front door. The plantings here are soft to provide a contrast—upright little bluestem grass, supple Japanese forest

PRECEDING SPREAD: Banks of Eupatorium Agha, Stachys, and Buddleja frame the outdoor living areas and infinity pool at the house's rear with a colorful pollinator haven. OPPOSITE: The front walk connects the house with the landscape by drawing visitors into the view. ABOVE: This landscape's created curves highlight the architecture's linear character.

ABOVE: There are countless ways to create invitation into a landscape. Here, a corridor of stone set into a gravel path proceeds between the guest house facade and a row of crape myrtles underplanted with Japanese forest grass. OPPOSITE: As the path begins to meander by a catalpa tree along a created rise, grass flows through its joints, and the beds become less formal.

grass, vertical crape myrtles, and some wildness on the other side of the driveway—yet they remain visibly in conversation with the man-made structures. To give the path that threads together the two houses a sense of play, grass interrupts the pavers, almost like a hop-scotch board. Here, a subtle grading makes the choreography feel almost inevitable.

At the back of the main house, an elegant expanse of glass, the indoor rooms transition to covered spaces, including the outdoor kitchen, which then unfold to the pool terrace with its dining and lounging areas that look across the pool to the lawn, meadows, pond, and wetlands beyond. From the wooden railing and fencing to the polished black granite of the pool walls to the grasses and butterfly bushes, which are both resistant to deer and incredibly attractive to butterflies, honeybees, and other pollinators, the detailing of the constructed elements reinforces the primary idea of this home: the architecture has been dropped into this idyllic natural setting. This extends to the pool area itself. Because this family includes many grandchildren, we designed a pool area that offers the option to lounge in three, nine, or twelve inches of water. With carefully planted Joe-Pye weed that reaches over the honed walls and almost enters the pool, it feels like nature is also on the move.

Within this man-made environment of water and stone, texture, form, color, fragrance, and motion captivate the senses from every vantage point on the property, ensuring this completely fabricated landscape of home feels simply meant to be.

RIGHT: In the summer, clients love living in those ambiguous, in-between, covered-yet-open spaces that allow them to be at one with both the architecture and the landscape. These various seating areas are this house's response to that desire. The result of true design collaboration, they flow organically from the house and into one another.

TOP, LEFT TO RIGHT: Layered gardens encircle the pool house. The pool terrace of Madras Grey sandstone sits eighteen inches below the other terraces to allow views of monarch butterflies on the Eupatorium purpureum Gateway. Crape myrtles underplanted with Japanese forest grass filter light beautifully onto the guest house walkway. ABOVE, LEFT TO RIGHT: Various pollinator plantings including Joe-Pye weed, Agastache, verbena, Buddleja, and white salvia create a setting for the pool.

OLD TREES

Nature sometimes works her marvels in the most mysterious ways, which is why the delight of discovery factors so profoundly into every aspect of what we do. So it was with this property, from the very first time we walked the site through the entire collaborative process of its design and creation with the interior design firm of Haynes-Roberts.

Here, both nature and human needs and desires presented us with unique opportunities and exceptional challenges. This was the second property we were creating for this family as they continued to grow. Because the site was legally two lots, the landscape had to take on the starring role in bringing the separate parts together into a coherent, unified whole.

We found the entire parcel, part of which had been home to another family for generations, rooted with a library of botanical wonders: magnificent copper beeches, majestic old maple and plane trees, one-hundred-fifty-year-old Japanese maples, fabulous Japanese cypresses, towering cryptomerias—all old-growth stalwarts, so full of soul and so unexpected on a property that is inland, but still comparatively near the coast. In our first meeting, we decided unanimously that we had no choice but to allow these trees to be the guiding element in our scheme for developing the design. We would preserve the existing old shingle-style family house, but move it to another location on the property, updating it with expanses of glass to

PRECEDING SPREAD: These existing ancient maples were the starting point for this home's design.
ABOVE: Old-growth trees and shrubs give the landscape of this home its distinctive character.
OPPOSITE TOP: Boxwood and privet hedges create a layered cushion between the gravel entry and the house. OPPOSITE: The arrival sequence flows organically off the main entry stair of the house.

connect the interior and exterior. We also decided to create a new guest house to welcome children and grandchildren.

Buildings, roads, pool, tennis court—we positioned every feature and detail of this property to celebrate the trees as the dominant force on this landscape, for they give it its remarkable character, and, if you will, its ineffable soul. Massive, strong, indelible, the trees act as connector and divider between the main house and the guest house for the younger generations, providing wonderfully cooling shade in the summer months with a greensward swept under and around them. The pool and the tennis court create their own rooms along one end of the property so as not to interrupt the kingdom of trees at the center of the site.

One of the knottier challenges the site handed us was the question of what to do with a fabulous rank of hundred-year-old, rosy, elegant rhododendrons. We had to preserve them because they were irreplaceable. Yet we had to move the house that was immediately adjacent. When we were told that they would

ABOVE, OPPOSITE: This property's existing old-growth trees, which give the landscape so much character, created a framework for all the decision-making about where to site structures, play spaces, and gardens. OVERLEAF: The vista from the pool area, enclosed by simple cedar picket fences, stretches across the main lawn to the guest house. The geranium Rozanne and white echinacea that flank one side of the gate with blossoms give way to Buddleja on the other, a pollinator's Eden.

have to go or we couldn't transplant the house, we decided to tunnel under the rhododendrons, digging down two feet to slip in steel plates beneath their root systems (rhododendrons have fairly shallow roots) for support. Then we excavated further, inserting steel beams underneath the plates to carefully extricate and move the house. Today, the rhododendrons are happy, healthy, and do not miss the old house that used to cozy up next to them. Yet they remain beacons still, seemingly ageless guides to the front door of the new home for visitors and family alike.

TOP, LEFT TO RIGHT: Crape myrtle, hydrangea, and grasses create an evolving backdrop for the pool area. This century-old stand of rhododendrons was irreplaceable. Crape myrtle and hydrangea show off their contrasting characters. ABOVE, LEFT TO RIGHT: The guest house's firepit nests into a low stone wall built to protect an existing tree. This walk connects the pool area to the great lawn. Poolside lounging is one of summer's great perks.

ART GARDEN

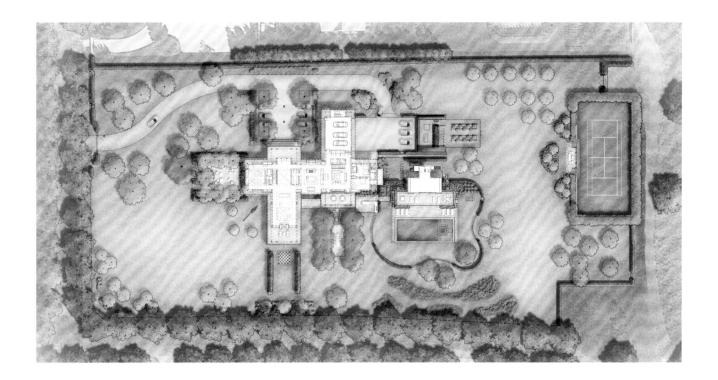

Each home is unique by definition, the offspring of a singular marriage between the site, the clients, and the collaborators. That said, a project like this one, which we designed together with James Merrell Architects and Kelly Behun Studio, redefined the notion of exceptionalism because its particulars encouraged all of us to think differently. The young owners wanted not simply a family home with plenty of outdoor areas for activities and fun, but a family home in which art is essentially the prime mover, and thus integral to the overall design, inside and out.

The property, a post-agricultural site, was reasonably flat with hedges on four sides. The contemporary architecture of the house incorporated significant expanses of glass. We took it as a given that the goal was to knit together the interior and exterior, which called on us to translate the architecture's spare forms, axial relationships, and emphasis on views into the outdoor spaces.

From the start, we wanted to devise a plan that set and framed each artwork as perfectly as possible, and that incorporated the individual pieces and the overall collection into unified composition. Our goal was to create a home for the sculpture and the family, not an art park. Deriving the landscape's geometry from the shapes, forms, and lines of the architecture was important for congruity. So was taking cues for the hardscape materials from the architecture's neutral palette. Orienting the exterior rooms off the interior's primary spaces was a must

PRECEDING SPREAD: Kelly Behun designed the chess set off the living room; Thomas Heatherwick's spinning stool adds to the whimsy. Pleached Carpinus trees underplanted with lavender, Russian sage, allium, Kalimeris, and anemone frame this space as a pollinator's haven.
ABOVE: The landscape design introduces twenty-five types of trees. OPPOSITE TOP: Honey locusts in the entry court provide shade for people and food for pollinators. OPPOSITE: Potted hydrangea and a hedge of Pennisetum grasses take the edge off the entry's formal geometry.

for the seamless transitions of an effortless indoor-outdoor lifestyle. Yet just as key was that the landscape also capture and express the family's playful, sophisticated spirit.

We knew to keep various sculptures in mind at the outset of planning. And we adjusted throughout the process to feature additional works as they entered the collection. One of the great muses was a chess set with furniture-sized pieces that we framed by a lawn and surrounded by plain hornbeam hedges and gardens with high-contrast plantings. This area sits on a direct axis with the house's main living area; the spatial and visual relationships enhance the sheer wit in the connection. This intersection of art and nature repeats across the property. The idea of sculpture even animates more typical elements of the landscape, like the sweeping stainless steel picket that guards the swimming pool, then swoops down, disappears into a perimeter hedge, and reemerges as if out of the blue.

Yet the family comes first, so along with the chess garden, the landscape also embraces a moon garden, an alfresco garden, a pool area, orchards, vegetable gardens, and play spaces. There's a butterfly meadow, for example, that grows as high as five feet. Filled with Joe-Pye weed, hibiscus, and other pollinator flowers, it has become almost a meadow maze for the kids, one that leads out to an adventure playground.

Perhaps more than any other, this home juxtaposes the expected and the unexpected in an original idiom of art, nature, and design.

RIGHT: The curving fence with round stainless steel pickets becomes a curving hedge at points as it encircles the pool. A Chinese fringe tree (at left) doubles as a natural chandelier in the evening with the addition of hanging lanterns by Kelly Behun.

RIGHT: Indoor space transitions easily to outdoor space at the pool house thanks to the close collaboration with James Merrell Architects. Madras Grey sandstone surrounds the pool. The spa floats in the middle of the pool's shallow end to invite lounging.

58

RIVER VIEW

The Hudson Valley is a uniquely storied region steeped in rich history, fabulous geology, with a complex ecology, all of which have been written about and depicted in paintings for centuries: the magic of thunderstorms rolling up the Hudson River, of sunsets over great groves of trees that seem to burst into flame as they turn orange and yellow in the fall, of dense, tangled wilderness leading up to dramatic cliffs. The goal of this project was to capture the full panoply of the valley's wonderments on a site resplendent with majestic trees and magnificent views across the river. Our task, working collaboratively with Steven Holl Architects, was to create a family home that evinced a harmonious marriage between a rolling site populated with great trees, where the geology was asserting itself, and organically elegant modern structures placed poetically to make the most of the property and its views. The building architecture informed all our decisions in terms of style, materials, and design of the constructed landscape, while the geology and existing trees were our guide for the living landscape. Our team collaborated intensively with the architects to ensure that each facet of our design for the landscape, individually and collectively, reflected the modern geometric forms of the buildings.

PRECEDING SPREAD: A strategic effort to preserve the spirit of place included carefully protecting a magnificent existing willow oak and towering fernleaf beech. ABOVE: This landscape reflects the elements of its architecture, both man-made and natural. OPPOSITE TOP: Irregular polygonal black basalt pavers break apart erratically beneath the stately specimens. OPPOSITE: Linear basalt risers and turf treads traverse the terraced hillside.

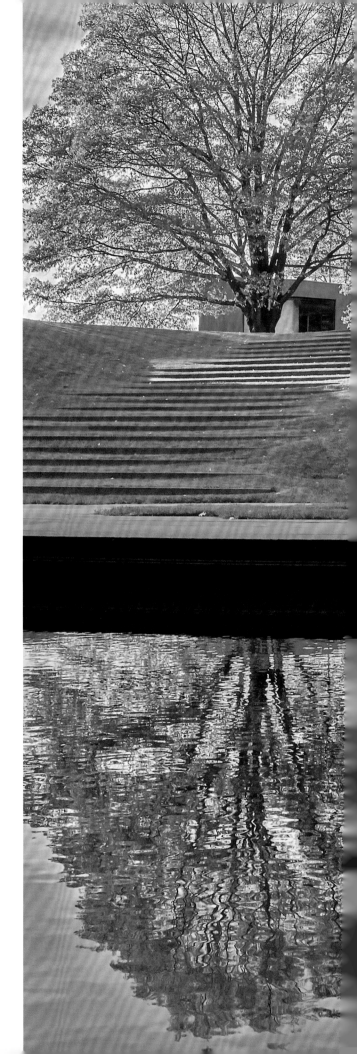

Because the structures are rigorous in line and spare in detail, the landscape is equally measured in the detailing of all its elements. We choreographed the aspects of invitation and orientation into the design, laying out the entry procession to draw this family and their friends through the trees to the front of the house and pull them into the views through the house to the Hudson River and the horizon beyond. Our built vocabulary mirrors the architecture in its strict lines and overlapping angular forms. The pathways that connect the home to the outbuildings bisect the site yet integrate with the natural rise and fall of the topography as they lead through and among the property's regal bosques of great old trees.

PRECEDING SPREAD: Salvaged wisteria vines grow on trellises along the concrete retaining wall. Four-, five-, or six-sided basalt pavers laid out in a nonrepeating pattern converge into walkways that zigzag through the ginkgo grove and down a slope to the pool house. RIGHT: In a double vision, the poolside view reflects the landscape atop the bluff.

TOP, LEFT TO RIGHT: Analogous to the talus slopes at the cliff base, no two stones are alike. These walkways negotiate eighteen feet of grade change. Linear risers appear to pin and stabilize the hillside. ABOVE, LEFT TO RIGHT: Willow fronds weep into the light. Pavers appear to break erratically. In autumn, ginkgo leaves mottle walkways with glints of gold.

ON THE POND

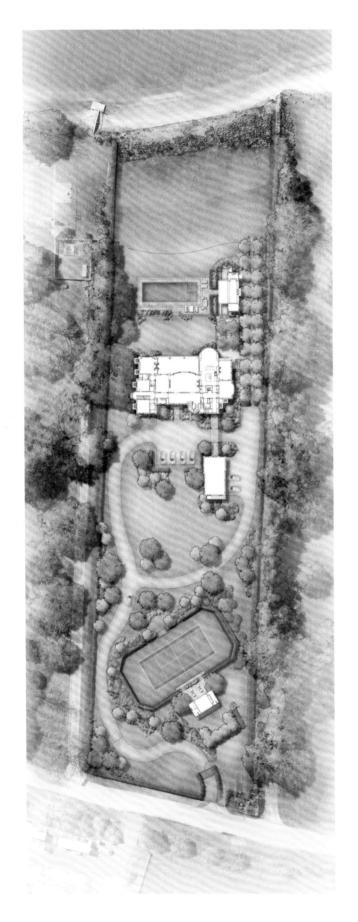

rees have been the landscape architect's best friend through history, for they endow any site where they thrive with the kind of character it can only gain across the generations of their growth. This property, a long narrow piece of land on a beautiful coastal pond, was rich in that beneficence of arboreal grandeur. The young family wanted us, together with Peter Pennoyer Architects, to create a modern home utilizing traditional architecture that felt as though it could have been there forever. Our task was to figure out how to figure out the routes to the house, the tennis court, and the swimming pool. More importantly, we were charged with creating outdoor living areas that expressed the family's capacity for surprise, delight, and adventure.

As a result, the landscape reflects this desire to enjoy life. To spend time with family and friends. To have spaces where they can engage and entertain, whether sharing a meal under the trees of the dining terrace, relaxing under the pergola at the pool house, or sitting on the lawn overlooking the pond and watching the sunset.

Rather than passing through the typical gate at the street, the act of entry becomes an act of discovery that happens at a remove, farther up the drive. Once through the gate, the drive proceeds, winding its way under two majestic old plane trees as though it had been there forever. The crunch of the gravel under the tires—that soft, soothing sound that signifies home—starts to reduce the blood pressure. It never

PRECEDING SPREAD: The layers of boxwoods, rhododendrons, magnolias, plane trees, and crab apples that frame the entry court help give this property its ageless quality. LEFT: All the design decisions prioritized making this new home feel timeless. OPPOSITE TOP: Setting the entry gate away from the road enhances the discovery. OPPOSITE: At the front door, the plantings open their arms in welcome.

ceases to amaze that with something as mundane as the layout of a driveway in a soft circuitous route, we can celebrate a site's existing trees and its peaceful, pastoral character. Here, we added groves of katsura trees as well as Japanese silver bells, crab apples, cherries, and plane trees—all trees with seasonal presence that welcome spring, flower during the summer, and turn orange, yellow, and bronze in the fall—so the landscape would be always alive and inviting.

Broad bluestone terraces at the back of the house beckon with places to sit and enjoy the cool summer breezes. A tantalizing allée of crape myrtles lined with hydrangea and astilbe gives a peekaboo view down to the pond and acts as a draw toward the water, where a kayak or paddleboard awaits. At night, when the lights come on, the tree trunks dance and the spaces take on a more magical tone. Cafe lights twinkle in the overstory of the four plane trees that shelter the graveled dining terrace, where the sunset across the pond casts enchantment and provides a reminder to cherish the moment and enjoy how wonderful life can be. The lawns roll down to a meadow of native milkweeds, grasses, and wildflowers that buffer the pond and create a habitat for the birds, bees, and butterflies that also call this site home.

With traditional forms and materials, we created an environment that does not shout, but rather welcomes all who enter and makes them feel not simply comfortable, which is wonderful, but at home, which is even better.

RIGHT: An allée of crape myrtles underplanted with Blushing Bride hydrangea, geranium Rozanne, and various white astilbe heighten the experience of walking to the coastal pond.
FOLLOWING SPREAD: At the dining terrace, carefully choreographed lighting overhead and in the surrounding plantings creates a magic mood for dinners alfresco.

RIGHT: Large slabs of bluestone frame the pool simply, yet elegantly. The dark bottom of the pool allows the water surface to reflect the sky. A low stone wall separates the rear terrace lawn from the pool area; beyond the pool, the lawn gives way to low meadow grass and, ultimately, the wetland meadow that embraces the pond.

FUN HOUSE FARM

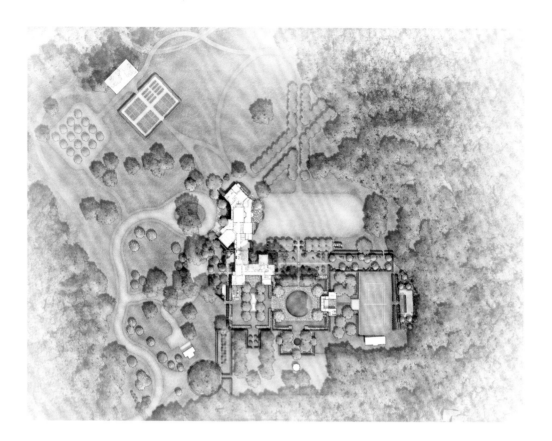

How do you design a landscape for laughter and joy? With care, with imagination, and with these very special clients, who love to cook, dine, entertain, and play, and who revel in the happy chaos of life that ensues with kids, dogs, and friends. Add into the mix an unusual property that's off the beaten track in the piney woods, a house in need of renovating, and ten-plus acres of grounds, gardens, and meadows in want of rethinking.

This couple wanted to be involved with the planning, maintenance, and all facets of the property design because they enjoy getting out into the garden and into the landscape. For architectural inspiration, they worked with Jeffery Povero and his team and looked to Coney Island in its heyday to bring a sense of irony to the details. They insisted on a landscape that was ecologically appropriate, with plenty of places for indoor-outdoor life and a huge vegetable garden, a potager or kitchen garden, stands of berry bushes, and an orchard of fruit trees. The property, as a result, is a fascinating balance of landscape structure; areas for fun, play, and entertaining; natural expanses; secret rooms and destinations; and a working farm. The axial alignments we organized to create coherence are softened by all sorts of wildish plantings loved by the birds, butterflies, and bees.

The property had many old bones that we wanted to salvage. Our task was to put vivacious new flesh on them in a way that suited the current, lively owners. The idea of a

PRECEDING SPREAD: An allée frames a shady path that provides new definition to the preexisting grand lawn. Low stone walls throughout the landscape were preserved or repurposed. ABOVE: Much of the plan involved creating axial alignments for coherence, comfort, and views. OPPOSITE: The entry drive eases around existing pines. The fescue and clover meadow that replaced the front lawn reduces the need for chemicals and provides a healthy area for pollinators.

RIGHT: A blend of three grasses in fescue sod creates a soft counterpoint to the sculptured boxwoods, hedges, and arborvitae in the topiary garden, where whimsical statuary hares play hide and seek.

ABOVE: Soft plantings, garden gates, and amusing garden follies and statues play a significant design role in this landscape, doing much to convey its sense of mystery, fun, and surprise. OPPOSITE: An unexpected peekaboo moment, one of many that occur throughout the property, provides a through-the-looking-glass spark of joy and humor.

round pool fifty feet in diameter became a—really, *the*—defining feature of the design because it fit their idea of home perfectly and allowed us to center the axial pathways that helped us to blend the existing with the new.

The centerline of the house comes through the exterior dining area, which we flanked with elms; we added a huge outdoor kitchen immediately adjacent. We extended this axis through a pergola surrounded with panel gardens all the way to bocce and shuffleboard courts. Another vector starts at the fountain courtyard and travels across the pool, through a wall (one of many we rebuilt or added), then along the existing row of pruned little leaf lindens to a series of fabulous small rooms we enriched with boxwoods, long grasses, and paths. Throughout, we carefully edited the existing landscape, saving old specimens to serve as a counterpoint to our new plantings.

Still another trajectory crosses the circular pool from the diving board to a cabana that resembles a changing room at Coney Island in the 1950s. Beyond the cabana, we planted a butterfly garden of pollarded catalpa trees carpeted with calamintha, Russian sage, and eupatorium that unfolds to a set of stairs leading to the top of an existing earth-form amphitheater.

Every axis we created draws people deeper into the landscape, whether it's a path lined with river birch that marches through the meadow or a new allée off the primary bedroom that points into the distance.

Is this landscape whimsical, eccentric, and magical? Absolutely. It's also full of fun and laughter.

RIGHT: In the aptly named Seuss Garden Walk, pollarded catalpa trees recall truffula trees. The full sensory garden beneath grows along an undulating turf path. Native and naturally adapted plants invite birds and butterflies. The property's beehives make use of this pollinator garden, too. FOLLOWING SPREAD: An allée of elm trees and fastigiate sweetgums embrace the dining terrace.

ABOVE: The new pool, fifty feet in diameter, nests within a bluestone terrace surrounded by panels of hydrangea and flowering perennials. OPPOSITE: With its centerline reorganized, the renovated house now lines up with the amphitheater, a dominant force in the surroundings. A new allée (seen at top left) provides greater definition to the amphitheater's lawn, as does the addition of meadow along the berms, which also provides a staging area for more of the property's whimsical sculpture.

TOP, LEFT TO RIGHT: Bluestone pavers mark one of the property's dramatic axes. The renovated fountain anchors another. Hydrangea hedges screen the outdoor shower. Rectilinear and irregular bluestone pavers reoccur throughout.
ABOVE, LEFT TO RIGHT: Sculptures add charm to the outdoor kitchen. Light-strung trees shelter the dining terrace. Pollarded catalpas ensure the Seuss Garden Walk resembles its namesake. The firepit is a connecting node in the landscape.

HIGHLAND MEADOWS

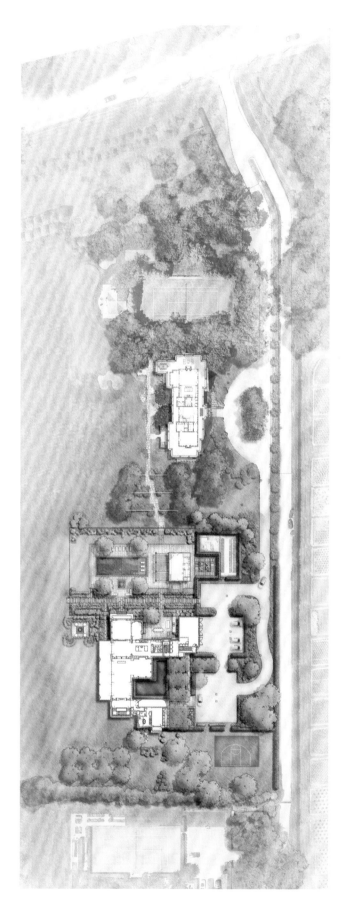

Every property is in its own way an expression of time. This one celebrates its post-agricultural landscape and unfolds from its refocused center of gravity, a new main house by architects Kligerman Architecture & Design with interiors by Haynes-Roberts. With fifteen acres, there was ample space to carve out areas for the family to swim and to play tennis, pickleball, basketball, and baseball, and even to hit golf balls. We modified the design of the existing pool area to harmonize with the new main house, and fashioned the connections from place to place, from inside to out, to create welcoming, functional areas, both covered and uncovered, for outdoor living and dining.

Given the site's great scope and scale, we were able to create generous transitions into the property's farther reaches. The lawns open to a wildflower meadow, which then unfolds into an orchard, stands of raspberry and blueberry bushes, and a previously underutilized area of the property that we were fortunate to have, and that we put to work growing many of the trees we used in the construction and planting of the landscape.

The entry sequence to the front door proceeds past plantings that hide the former main house, now the guest house. As it nears the front of the house, it magnifies and enhances the back-and-forth play among the architecture, landscape, and interiors, which, because of our close collaboration, all sing together in one choir. The pared-down, traditional shingle-style house features

PRECEDING SPREAD: A tranquil reflecting pool at this home's entrance blurs the distinction between land and water. LEFT: Pastoral views of an agricultural preserve on site guided many design decisions. OPPOSITE TOP: A low hedge of green velvet boxwood contains Japanese anemone that bloom white in the spring. OPPOSITE: Black Mexican pebbles at the base of the water feature help with reflectivity and create places for pollinators to perch.

RIGHT: The water feature also has a spillway (just visible through the anemone) so water is constantly moving, keeping it fresh without the need for lots of chemicals. The sound of the moving water also attracts pollinators and birds to the space.

very contemporary interiors, a combination that called for a highly structured, architectural front landscape to introduce this complexity of opposites. The entry occurs along a covered walkway, with passage through a bosque of pollarded plane trees growing out of beds of Japanese anemone. These are set along a large reflecting pool within a black steel frame surrounded by a plinth of green boxwood. This water feature mirrors not just the flat forms of the architecture, but also the simplicity of its details, including the black-edged windows that offer views straight through the house.

The fronts of houses tend to be places of transition and movement, of invitation and introduction, while the backs tend to be places for meditation and relaxation, enjoyment and gathering. For moving to the back of this house—and going from public to private—we developed a sequence of transitional spaces leading to places that people occupy. The primary one—a pathway bordered by crisp plantings of grasses, lavender, and Hydrangea paniculata Bombshell, tailored to reflect the simplicity of the architecture and with a color mix that juxtaposes beautifully with the house's cedar shingles—bypasses the house altogether so friends can come straight through to the pool and backyard. The swimming pool, like the reflecting pool in the front, is built with a rimless edge that helps transform it into a mirror, which brings the sky and the earth into the same plane. It basks in the shade of four large plane trees that also provide architectural definition.

As reimagined for this family, this home lives in the landscape as much as it does in the architecture.

RIGHT: An allée of Phenomenal lavender and Little Lime hydrangea borders the path to the backyard and leads visitors straight to the pool. OVERLEAF: The pool house complex, cornered by four large plane trees, anchors the outdoor living areas and creates a transitional experience between the very contemporary home and the more traditional guest house.

TOP, LEFT TO RIGHT: An ilex hedge frames the service court. A grove of clump catalpa trees grown at the property's on-site nursery is underplanted with Carex. ABOVE, LEFT TO RIGHT: Pollinator gardens connect the main and guest houses. In the evening, soft lighting envelopes the poolside. The entry walk of Madras Grey pavers centers the view past green velvet boxwoods to mature weeping willows.

COUNTRY CLASSIC

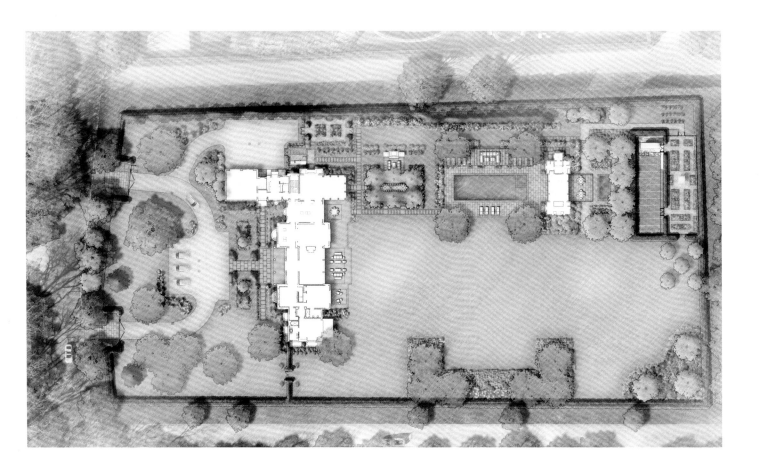

When the entire team and the clients agree on what transforms the blank canvas that is a property into the landscape of home, it's a recipe for magic. This young family with European sensibilities envisioned their summer home as a fresh take on traditional design. Our collaborators here, Ferguson & Shamamian Architects and Victoria Hagan Interiors, share our convictions on how to parlay design's classical principles—beckoning entries that make orientation clear; driveways that feel inevitable; houses that reveal themselves; and landscapes that unfold in outdoor rooms and spaces—into homes that celebrate the family.

Because this property lives within a village setting, the plots are parceled and the neighbors are close. To make the most of the available expanses in the preferred vocabulary, the drive spools graciously into an entry court marked by a magnificent existing copper beech, which we mirrored with a new grove of copper beeches in the back. The entry proceeds ceremonially through two great hornbeams and up a gravel stepping-stone walk to the front of the house and mudroom door.

Directly off the back of the house, a series of terraces relates intimately to the indoor rooms. These lead to the enfilade of pool, pool house, and reflecting

PRECEDING SPREAD: Bluestone pavers lead the way through a pair of towering hornbeams to the entry court and front door, where another stone pathway turns off to the side kitchen. ABOVE: Symmetry was key to this property's design. OPPOSITE: Gaura and white Annabelle hydrangea arch over grass-jointed stepping stones that connect the rear terrace to the swimming pool.

pool garden, aligned axially down the property's north side. A stepping-stone path framed by Gaura, hydrangea, and geranium Rozanne provides the invitation into the landscape. It arrives first at the dining terrace, nested beneath the canopy of six enchantingly lit plane trees, adjacent to a furnished exterior parlor and outdoor fireplace. Pink, blue, and purple hydrangea frame these spaces with color, while native pea gravel within a bluestone border adds a lovely crunch underfoot. The walkway then proceeds to the pool area, classic in green and white, where white hydrangea, white roses, and white butterfly bushes glow as the sun sets and sparkle in the evening light. Beyond the pool house is the fountain garden, essentially a reflecting pool in a sea of fragrant lavender and roses, a perfect casual spot for an alfresco meal. And past that is the vegetable garden.

On the property's south side, we sowed a pollinator meadow with grasses and wildflowers that dance in the breeze and change color and texture from summer through fall. This arrangement left us with a great expanse of lawn—the living room, as it were. For symmetry, on axis with the centerline of the pool area and pergola, we planted a bosque of horse chestnut trees that explode into big white blooms in summer's height.

We designed this landscape to be inhabited around the summer clock. Its variety gives all who spend time in it countless options for delight.

PRECEDING SPREAD: A Madras Grey sandstone terrace surrounds the swimming pool; the stone color and plantings that create the lush green and white borders harmonize with the furnishings selected by Victoria Hagan. RIGHT: A bosque of plane trees arches over the dining terrace, which flows into the lounge area around the fireplace.

TOP, LEFT TO RIGHT: The sunroom garden looks to the dining bosque. A breakfast nook anchors the pool walkway. An axial relationship unites the dining area, pool, pool house, and reflecting garden. TOP, LEFT TO RIGHT: Natchez crape myrtles and lavender frame the reflecting pool with texture, color, and scent. Hedges of Endless Summer hydrangea define the gravel dining bosque. A pollinator meadow borders the property.

LINDEN HILL

Nature has her own mysterious poetry of placement. At this property, set in a classic summer cottage village, she gifted us with magnificent, century-old fernleaf beeches, copper beeches, and lindens. Such old-growth trees, so unusual in a salt-air setting, endow this place with its essential character, drama, and feeling. Our goal, working alongside architect Tom Kligerman, was to create a new home and landscape within the framework presented by the trees. The challenge was taking advantage of them as focal points of the composition without injuring them during the construction process. This meant working within very strict spatial parameters.

Two majestic fernleaf beeches formed a natural gateway to begin the procession to the front of the house, so entry to the property is beneath their bows. At the back of the house, the overstory of a beautiful old linden became the sheltering sky for a dining terrace immediately beyond the screened porch; throughout the day, but especially at night, it becomes a place of enchantment. We offset the pool area and tennis court along one side of the property so they wouldn't impinge on the sweep of the lawn that rolls into the majestic trees. Anchored by a pool house that overlooks and becomes part of yet another garden, the raised, rimless pool reflects the evanescent light, clouds, and mist in the ever-shifting sky like a magic mirror. The choreography of the connections and transitions across the property, along with their materials, evolve from the more natural to the combination of natural and man-made to the fully man-made as they approach the house.

PRECEDING SPREAD: Stairs built into a remnant dune blend together the site architecture and landscape; the framing allée of pleached lindens heightens the rhythm of the experience. RIGHT: Determining the best, most careful way to insinuate the drive safely between the property's magnificent fernleaf beeches was an involved process.

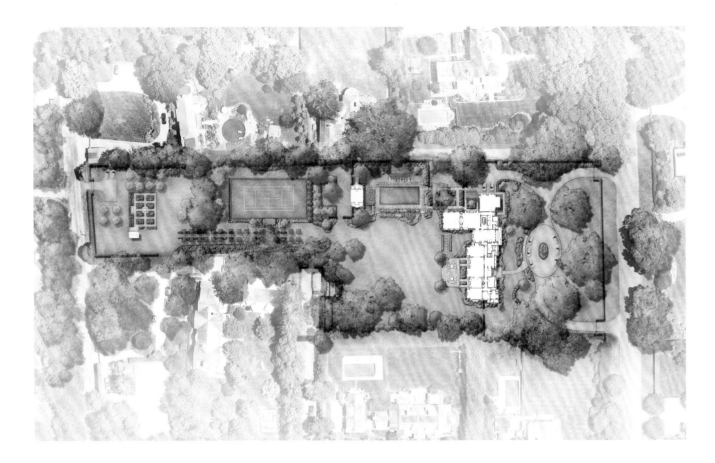

The defining feature of the site's topology—a remnant ancient sand dune, long overgrown and stabilized by the vegetation that grows on and around it—separates the property's front from its back. To connect these two areas, we composed an allée of pleached linden trees to frame stone slab stairs that traverse the geological relic, centered as if by wizardry on the primary interior living room, and organized moments of discovery in the various views along the way. At night, carefully placed lights offer clear direction and dramatic shadow play.

The back of the property—called the farm—brings home another kind of bounty with its newly planted orchard of apple, pear, and peach trees; blueberry and raspberry bushes; and garden of heirloom tomatoes, eggplants, and cucumbers.

So much of what we do involves shaping the elements to provide instants of anticipation, surprise, and destination. These experiences give this home its unique identity: lounging and dining outside with family and friends, strolling across the lawn, enjoying the swimming pool and tennis court, or whizzing through the landscape on zip lines in the trees. On the stairs in the linden allée, there's the mood of movement and enclosure. On the big open lawn, there's the pull of freedom, and running, and openness. In the gardens, fragrance, color, and texture beckon. And in the evening, under the big linden tree, peace and tranquility reign. Delighting each of the senses differently in every area of the property creates an unforgettable landscape of home.

ABOVE: The property's abundant, diverse, and glorious existing trees guided many of the team's design decisions.
OPPOSITE: Expressions of invitation create a sense of delight in a garden. The paving is New York State bluestone.

ABOVE AND OPPOSITE: Functionality and aesthetics combine in the ultimate design of the route traversing the site. In the materials underfoot, the pathway to the house reflects the sequence of changes from open space to shaded rise (grass wants full sun). FOLLOWING SPREAD: Carefully positioned lights illuminate the linden-lined stairway when dusk falls. Hydrangea and wisteria screen views of the tennis court.

HOME BY THE SEA

A maritime environment has its own special kind of magic. Salt gives the air a piquant tang that whets the appetite and enhances sleep. The light changes from hour to hour all year long as it refracts off clouds, filters through fog and mist, and reflects off the water. The colors of the sky transform continually from before dawn until after dusk throughout the cycle of the seasons. All these conditions, wondrous and dramatic as they are, affect the landscapes of home we create along the coast from Nantucket to the Hamptons, from the Caribbean to Montecito.

Geology, hydrology, soils, and vegetation: these are site-specific to a given locale. In combination, they define each place and endow it with a unique identity. There are obvious ecological implications to designing and constructing architecture and landscapes that are exposed to, and at the mercy of, the full force and power of Mother Nature. It is really she who shapes the distinctive forms of the coastal areas—the shores, sounds, bays, marshes, estuaries, and wetlands—with sun, wind, salt, storms, and tides. Salt, in and of itself, is remarkable. All living things need it to survive, and yet it is incredibly destructive.

Because coastal environments can be so harsh, successful coastal landscapes answer to their parameters. Our designs for the water side of a property tend to differ from those on its leeward side simply because of greater exposure to wind, salt, and other stressors. We always embrace the majesty of the views, which, by definition, are expansive. We inevitably include outdoor places to sit, dine, entertain, recreate, contemplate, and relax. And we always emphasize, above all, topography, sweeping vistas, magical light, and textural play, and plant life that moves in the breeze and stands up to the soils and Mother Nature's various whims.

Rarely, if ever, do coastal properties include the kinds of great old trees that grace the countryside. The closer we get to the ocean, the more stressful the environment and the greater the economy of means in terms of plants available for our palette. When we get to the oceanfront itself, the options are very limited. Inland, of course, we have more flexibility.

Landscapes by the sea are sculpted by the sea. Every choice we make responds to this reality.

OPPOSITE: There is nothing more beautiful or harsher than a maritime environment. Wind, sea, salt—all the elements that make the beach one of nature's wonderlands—sculpt and buffet absolutely everything.

DUNE HOUSE

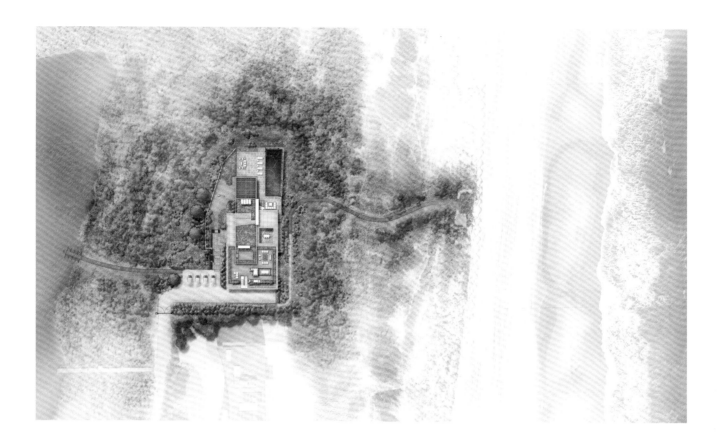

There is no challenge quite like trying to create a jewel box in a natural landscape already as beautiful as can be imagined. This site is a remarkable intersection of ocean, pond, dune, wetlands, wildlife, and sea, sky, light, and air. Wherever you are on the property, you feel at one with the world. Collaborating with Leroy Street Studio and Victoria Hagan, we wanted to create a modern home that celebrated art made by man, and that honored and preserved the art of nature.

A site like this comes with numerous constraints, ecological and otherwise. In creating the outdoor spaces, we had to merge art, science, and constructability, to blend what's desired with what's required in terms of the necessary infrastructure for this kind of house in this type of ecologically sensitive environment.

The walkway to the front of the house climbs through a cascade of water because, with ponds on the north side and the ocean on the south, the site is about the aquatic. Along the boardwalk to the bay, we planted Joe-Pye weed, native hibiscus, and other native species that make even more magic of the wetland experience. For the boardwalk to the dunes, we innovated a new solution that resulted in a sensuous central byway to the beach. These boardwalks are typically either made of plastic grating or need to be elevated four feet above the dune with railings. But a close reading of the code revealed that the boardwalk had to be half open to

PRECEDING SPREAD: Uninterrupted views and thoughtfully selected materials make this home feel immersed in the landscape. The mezzanine's saltwater pool appears to float above the dunes. ABOVE: Environmental sensitivities informed each nuance of this design. OPPOSITE: The entry stair mimics the architecture's forms and materials. Cascading water adds joy to the climb and attracts birds and pollinators, as do bayberry, hydrangea, Buddleja, vitex, and Pennisetum.

allow enough air and light to sustain the beach grass below. We used curved ipe wood slats to create a transformative path to the beach that meets the half-open/half-closed mandate, ensures the journey is as special as the rest of the property, and preserves the health of the native beach grass community while gliding through the sinuous contours of the dune field.

Our goal with an oceanfront house like this is always to make the house feel at one with its setting, and maximize the places where the clients can feel as if they're in and of the ocean and the sky. Much of this house encompasses truly indoor-outdoor spaces, as do the transition areas between the interior and exterior rooms where the family can sit undercover, feel totally protected from the elements, yet smell the salt air, hear the waves hit the shore, and savor the breeze in all its moods.

The more extreme the environmental conditions are in a particular place, the more limited the palette of vegetation that wants to grow there. While our plantings here are not all strictly native, they are of the beach and adapted to these conditions, species like beach rose, beach plum, bayberry, and all sorts of native and ornamental grasses that feel soft and wild. There are also other florae, such as butterfly bush (Buddleja), that thrive by the beach and attract butterflies, honeybees, hummingbirds, and other members of the universe that we want to welcome into the landscape for all sorts of reasons, not least because they enrich our lives.

ABOVE: Ipe slats allow the necessary flow of light and water in this boardwalk that connects the house and beach along the dune's sensuous curve. OPPOSITE: The exterior kitchen, dining area, pool, lounge, and yoga deck open seamlessly off corresponding interior rooms. With a black finish and black interior coping to enhance reflectivity, the pool mirrors its surroundings.

ABOVE: This breezeway, an in-between space that's both open to and protected from the elements, is the point of entry to the boardwalk. The sculpture is by Maya Lin. OPPOSITE: With a tight footprint dictated by building codes, the house brings the landscape into the living spaces and extends the living spaces into the landscape through clever framing that maximizes borrowed views.

PRECEDING SPREAD:
Constructing a wall between the new and native landscapes resolved the challenge of creating an art lawn on this site given its environmental sensitivities. Careful plant selections—bayberry, Eastern Baccharis, American elder, chokeberry, highbush blueberry, and Buddleja—help blur the boundary between the two areas; the plantings also tie together this garden and the front of the house. RIGHT: Consistent materials do much to unify the various outdoor rooms on separate levels of the house. Two types of dune grasses border a terrace raised above the lounge around the firepit to help tie that terrace into the landscape. Clean, simple, and unadorned, a retractable fabric "roof" shades the dining area as desired without obstructing the view.

GULLS' LANDING

There's a skill to listening to Mother Nature. We need to hear and respect her to make her our friend and partner. This was top of mind when we first walked this site with interior designer Bunny Williams and architect Douglas Wright, then at Hart Howerton. We found its groves of old trees and ocean views exceptional, but the existing house insufficient. Our task was to make the property, conceived as a multigenerational home, wonderful for now, with the flexibility to grow with the family in the future.

To create part of the landscape for today and part for what could be tomorrow, we began by identifying which trees would be in the way of the planned new construction, then moving these as necessary to give them new life. Over six months, we rechoreographed the entry, reshaping a prairie-like expanse into a sweep of gentle undulations by turning, softly grading, and sculpting the soil so that the new lay of the land would look designed by nature. The fifteen-hundred-foot-long drive now curves softly around great trees and through rolling terrain populated with sculptures. Swaths of meadows bloom with bulbs and wildflowers in the old fields leading to the house. From this emerges a great park with meadows, lawns, and groves of elms, lindens, and other tree species that, as they grow, will continue to transform the property.

To tie together the main house, guest house, and pool house, we cultivated a series of gardens, paths,

PRECEDING SPREAD: In the new rolling landscape, sculptures emerge among planted waves of ornamental grasses. ABOVE: Existing old-growth trees informed every aspect of this design. OPPOSITE TOP: Plantings along the pathways prioritize form, texture, and shades of green. OPPOSITE: Four transplanted Natchez crape myrtle trees underplanted with soft mountains of boxwoods, ivy, and magnolias shade the entry court.

and living areas with plants that revel in the setting: lavender, hydrangea, roses, wisteria, lindens, and many other trees, shrubs, and flowers that love salt and enjoy being sculpted by the wind. Stepping stones between lavender drifts thread together the main house and guest house. Green lanes of crape myrtles growing out of ivy and boxwoods join the main house to the site planned for a future guest house. A grove of ancient native black cherry trees underplanted by nature with a meadow of little bluestem was so perfect that we left it in place and then took credit for it. As the family expanded their property, we worked with Rees Jones and his team to create a golf course overlooking the ocean. Throughout, winding paths lined with black-eyed Susans, echinacea, bee balm, native maritime grasses, Buddleja, and vitex create a wonderland for both pollinators and humans.

The pool area was a true collaboration. Wisteria- and clematis-draped pergolas and paths banked by classic blue hydrangea ensure that the gardens, landscape, and architecture blend cohesively. Because roses thrive by the sea, we edged walkways in masses of blushing knockout shrub roses and trimmed an oval garden with white iceberg roses. All of this looks to the dunes and the ocean. The terrace that forms a border between the cultivated and the wild steps down to a wooden boardwalk that meanders through native cedars, bayberry, and shadblow before climbing the primary dune and landing on the beach and in Mother Nature herself.

RIGHT: This path connects the back of the house to the guest house; banks of lavender and peegee hydrangea trees add fragrance and color into the composition. OVERLEAF: The lavender here is meant to recall the waves of the ocean in the way the plants bow and dance in the breezes and come into staggered bloom.

RIGHT: Blushing knockout roses, which like all roses thrive by the sea, cushion the paved pathway to the pool in an abundance of blossoms, lush color, and intoxicating scent. The white iceberg roses rim an oval garden that balances the pool on the other side of the loggia while adding more interest and layers into the mix.

ABOVE, OPPOSITE: Black-eyed Susan, echinacea, bee balm, native maritime grasses, Buddleja, and vitex along winding turf paths between the guest house and golf course create wonderlands for pollinators and people. OVERLEAF: With golf course designer Rees Jones and his team, we preserved a grove of existing oaks and a maritime meadow as a buffer between the putting green and the ocean.

SEA BREEZES

Every home involves the intersection of architecture and landscape, but some homes, like this Florida residence, reflect this tenet of cohesiveness more than others. Largely created by interior designer Victoria Hagan in concert with the homeowners, the house consists of a series of pavilions, as is so often the case in the tropics. This is wonderful for landscape architects because it allows us to create a series of gardens that the buildings look out onto and open into—gardens that both separate and connect.

In warmer climates, gardens that become rooms for outdoor living tend to have seamless relationships with their corresponding indoor rooms. We generally extend the architectural axes into the landscape allowing the axial relationships—the exterior correlative to the interior enfilades—to determine the way we move not just from inside to outside, but from room to room in the landscape.

While the architecture of this house is not formal, it is highly tailored with clear geometric forms. We've softened the Euclidean presence of its built elements—its pads, walks, fences, and terraces, the places where family and friends live out of doors—with the lushness of the plantings. These are neither prim and precisely clipped nor untamed and fuzzy, but a happy marriage of the two, so the exterior feels inviting and soft, but also trim, well-shaped, and clean-lined.

PRECEDING SPREAD: Traditional parterre gardens inspired this landscape's orthogonal forms and defining hedges of Green Island ficus. Windswept coconut palms—some existing, some added—connect the beach to the house. ABOVE: Given the force of the elements along the oceanfront, the day-to-day outdoor living spaces occupy the property's leeward side. OPPOSITE: An allée of Sylvester palms turns the front entry into an occasion.

The views and vistas bring the property's disparate elements into cohesion. Shaping and framing the various sightlines and perspectives back and forth between inside and outside is such fun. The long panel of lawn on axis with the center of the pool is just one example of this byplay, as it appears to run through the pool house and out the back of the pool beyond.

We always fine-tune the elements of our designs, man-made and living, to the look and style our clients want to achieve, and to the architecture and interiors of their residence. When people love an environment that's soft and wild, that points us to one group of plants. If they prefer surroundings that are refined and elegant, we look to the options in a second group of plants. If their taste runs to the formal and geometric, we make selections from a third group of plants. It's critical to spend a great deal of time understanding local ecosystems and local growing patterns so that the world we create for each home is true to and right for the locale. No matter where you are, plantings, like the ones here, should be extremely site specific. Whether you're in St. Barts or Palm Beach, the Hamptons or Maine, what grows on the property—its living architecture—has to be adapted to its environment and to the seasonality of the house's use so it will look its best when it's on stage, so to speak.

RIGHT: Lower plantings define the outlines of an intermediate garden, called the cocktail lawn, outside the dining room, and provide floral interest. Above, multistemmed palms create an informal allée from the family room to the pool house, underscoring the axial alignment that plays such a defining role in this landscape.

TOP, LEFT TO RIGHT: Arrival at the motor court celebrates the ocean vista. Ferns, broadleaf plants, and orchid-studded trees lushly shade this perimeter path. Pool gardens emphasize shapes, scale, and forms that tie the landscape to the architecture. ABOVE, LEFT TO RIGHT: High and low plantings leave views unobstructed. A vestibule garden feels tropical with Christmas palms, jasmine, and planted pots. Christmas palms flank the pool house with relaxed symmetry.

WATER'S EDGE

So much of creating the landscape of home involves staging a drama of form, texture, color, and light on the canvas of the land as we find it. With BMA Architects and interior designers Fox-Nahem, we shaped a cohesive theater of place for this site that derives energy from contrast and difference, and especially from the way the landscape responds to, comments on, and integrates the built elements. The structures—a main house and an art barn, a studio space for artists to work and exhibit—are orthogonal. The lay of the land—two lots with great topographic variation—is curvilinear. We created corresponding groves of aspen and birch as unifying settings for the buildings. All the materials and plantings—exposed aggregate concrete; Corten steel for two sets of stairs,

planters, and an open picket pool fence; and gray foliage of artemisia at the front door—contribute to a family of contemporary influences appropriate for the design.

The main house extends to create a private courtyard on the ground level that opens to a gym and yoga deck, then steps up to a main floor with a connecting breezeway to the front door. There is also a covered dining and cooking terrace that looks out across a modernist pool designed to counterbalance the house's facade. Sculptures integrated into these areas help to reinforce this home's art-centric nature. We conceived the entire composition to bring the architecture and the site into balance.

Leaving the native oaks in place and creating a vista through the trees to the water allowed us to define

PRECEDING SPREAD: In form and texture, the plantings at the entry are part of a family of contemporary influences that speak to the materiality and language of the architecture. ABOVE: The plan's elements pull this property's two distinct sites into a unified whole. OPPOSITE: This stairway creates both a buffer and a connection between two wings of the building.

RIGHT: Another view of the stair between the building's wings gives some insight into the nature of the journey. Because there are twenty steps in total, but never more than three or four steps clustered together before the stair zigs or zags, the experience becomes a magical trip through a garden of river birch and Japanese forest grass with all sorts of twists and interesting vistas at every at every turn.

and emphasize the depths of foreground, midground, and background, which created three spaces out of one, giving the sweep of the landscape more character and interest. It also helped us highlight the transitions from built landscape to planted landscape to natural landscape. As the rise in the adjacent landscape begins, a series of curved Corten steel walls define and anchor a series of sand-filled, grass-covered plateaus that, planted with the river birch found in the rest of the property, traverse the hillside. A corresponding stair traverses the slope between the main house and a not yet completed guest house, a few steps at a time. It creates another ceremonial rite of passage out of a necessary transition with the same materials, treated differently.

Designed as a glass box, the art barn introduces art into nature and nature into art, the story of the entire property. The dark bottom of the pool mirrors the black walls of the structure. Between the horizontal surface of the pool and the vertical surface of the windows, some transparent, some reflective, there is a remarkable play of light, making the line between landscape and architecture seem to disappear. Under the overhang, the poolside area hosts an outdoor kitchen, dining lounge, and outdoor TV-viewing space. The oak trees, grasses, and bayberry—all native—create a relaxed aesthetic, and the perfect perch for a hammock.

When we began, the property was a dense thicket. With selective trimming, thinning, and pruning, the trees became the gateway from the the man-made to the wild. The topography with its variations influenced our choices. In the end, nature always makes its presence felt.

RIGHT: On one side, the perimeter of the pool takes cues from the form of the building; on the other, it transitions back to the landscape. The sculpture is by Nicole Eisenman. OVERLEAF: In a game of reflection and transparency, the pool and the windows play off one another to dramatic effect. Beyond the pool, a grove of existing oaks and a preserved maritime meadow provide a buffer beside the bay.

Part of the pool enclosure, the glass wall becomes an element of enchantment throughout the day as its appearance shifts in the changing light, temperature, and weather. The plantings of river birch trees that flow from the property's different houses create the landscape's connective tissue.

ABOVE, OPPOSITE: The transitions from built landscape to planted landscape to natural landscape are among a home's defining features. Here, the structures are orthogonal, and the landscape, curvilinear. Bowed Corten walls define the stepped terraces that traverse this slope; because each level is sand-filled, stormwater drains naturally back into the ground.

UNDER THE WIND

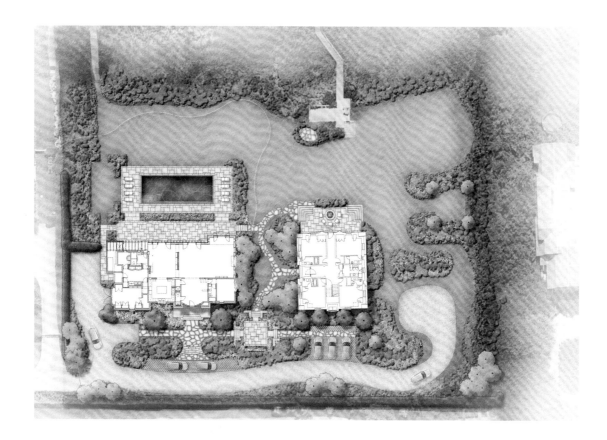

The ocean is the most powerful force on the planet, and it shapes everything around it, like this property that faces the Atlantic Ocean. Our design for the landscape here pays homage to the ocean's power, majesty, and beauty, while creating living areas for this family to enjoy. A collaboration with architects Kligerman Architecture & Design and interior designers Cullman & Kravis, this project has grown over the years. Because the building envelopes limited us to a degree, we thought out every detail to the individual stone.

Our design was an exercise in choreography, and in creating invitation, anticipation, and mystery. The layout of the main house made finding the front door a discovery, so we considered the materiality of the entry very carefully. No choice could be too precious or exacting, as we knew that the ocean would have her way with it. To cultivate harmony in the landscape, echo the relaxed nature of oceanside living, and complement the sun, wind, and breeze, we used informal bluestone stepping stones and a slightly wild, natural combination of crape myrtles, hydrangea, perennial flowers, and native grasses to subtly draw people to the front door.

The house had the feel of a ship at the ocean's edge, which meant our landscape was its dock. The back of the house spilled out to living and dining rooms; here we created a terrace area where the

PRECEDING SPREAD: Sod and cobble pavers combine to create an inviting drive court. ABOVE: Designed for multiple generations, this landscape balances open spaces for living and play with garden areas and sculpture. OPPOSITE: The layers and levels of salt-tolerant juniper, crape myrtles, and privet flanking the bluestone stairs make the approach to the front door increasingly enclosed and intimate.

family could enjoy lunches, dinners, and evening cocktails. Taking advantage of the variation in topography, we then descended a few steps to the swimming pool, which makes the pool area feel as if it's a different world. Intended as a major feature in the backyard, we designed it with a raised rimless edge so the water would look like a sheet of glass and act like a two-way mirror. From the house, it reflects everything that makes living on the ocean so magical; coming from the beach, it echoes the architecture of home.

As the project grew in scope and size, we had to determine how to bring the additional properties into the fold. The placement and materiality of the paths, walls, and parking areas became our means for tying the properties together and simultaneously rendering them distinct.

Working with the homeowners, design team, and art consultants to site the sculptures and create landscapes for each piece was fascinating. In a different kind of design dialogue, the sculpture became part of the landscape, and the landscape became part of the sculpture. We thought of the two as one, yet the conversation enriched the experience of both. And because sculpture played such an important role in the landscape, the bronze picket pool fence took on another dimension of meaning. Shaped by the rolling nature of the dunes, the curves of the fence reflect the way the dunes protect this property from the ocean and its shifting tides, while the fence serves as a work of art in its own right.

PRECEDING SPREAD: Nepeta, salvia, and Russian sage create a welcoming back garden designed specifically for the sculpture by Yayoi Kusama, which wittily makes itself at home. RIGHT: The bronze picket pool fence doubles as a sculptural element following the curves of the dunes, where beach grass blurs the edges.

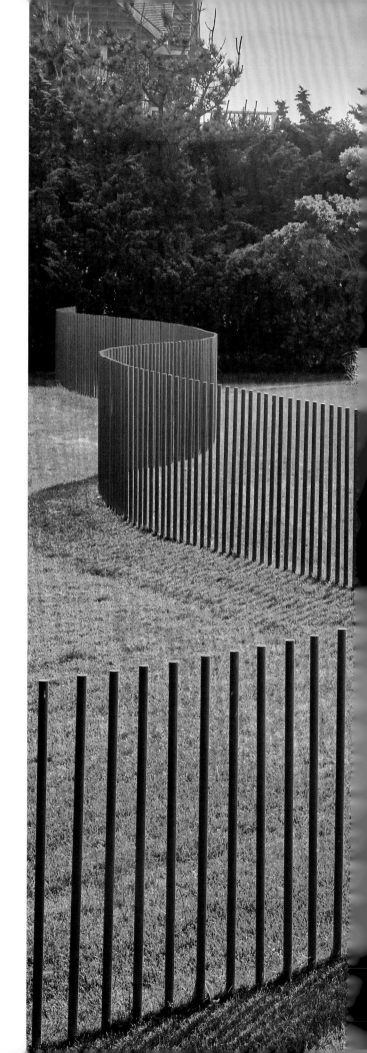

RIGHT: Chaise lounges sit on the short sides of the raised-edge pool to ensure that the views to the dunes and ocean from the home's interior remain unobstructed. A bed of Gaura Whirling Butterflies dances colorfully in the breezes at poolside, a softening natural element within the hardscape.

TOP, LEFT TO RIGHT: The fence's Corten pickets seem to hold nature in place. Sedum between bluestone pavers softens the path to the guest house terrace overlooking the sculpture garden. ABOVE, LEFT TO RIGHT: The path connecting the houses creates visual and functional continuity. The bluestone stair offers a timeless welcome. Native dune grasses, bayberry, and beach rose planted to stabilize the dune help protect the home from future storm surges.

ON THE BAY

Every piece of land possesses a unique poetry of place. For this site, it's the cadence and confluence of water, sky, and light, and the way in which these elements delight the senses. The property, which is home to a guest house/recreational building associated with the main house next door, is not especially large. With architects Kligerman Architecture & Design and interior designer Victoria Hagan, we created a landscape for privacy and play that celebrates life. Our work here blends the contemporary architecture with an essentially natural landscape into a refuge for the family with places to gather, dine, swim, and enjoy the gifts of the surroundings.

We start all our projects with the canvas that we find and develop all the desired elements of the home—pool, dining and living terraces, house, driveway—schematically. In this case, there were fabulous views combined with considerable environmental concerns. Our goal was to celebrate yet protect the sensitive wetland areas both within and bordering the site.

Sometimes these types of constraints make the overall challenge easier, because we have a framework to guide our thinking, inform our choices, and factor into our decision-making process. Here, a required drainage swale led us to devise the idea of the bridge that, literally and figuratively, now connects

PRECEDING SPREAD: The wetland meadow with milkweed, native grasses, and golden rod creates a buffer between the bay and the property's turf areas. ABOVE: This property's environmental opportunities and restrictions drove the planning of the landscape. OPPOSITE: The stone base of the house wraps around to create the stone wall of the pool's infinity edge.

the two properties and details a view to the wetland buffer area beyond.

There are design elements inside the house that pull the inside out and the outside in, and they are not simply the covered and uncovered living areas that provide transitions into the outdoors. The slight curve on the back of the pool, for example, reflects a shape that goes all the way through from the interior to the architecture to the terraces and our designs for the landscape, all of which focus on the bay. Details make a difference, from the placement of the various terraces to capture the short, mid, and long views to the bay to the ipe wood deck set into the stone that steps down to the pool.

The pool, incredibly elegant and very complex to build, combines a rimless edge with an infinity edge. This kind of rimless-edge pool is designed so the surface of the pool is coplanar, and turns into a mirror, a reflector of the magic created by light and moisture; the sun refracts off mist and clouds, the bay, the shifts in the sky from sunrise to sunset, and everything else in the surroundings.

Our goal with our collaborators always is to ensure that all the property's different living areas look as if they were designed by one set of hands, because all our hands were involved in every space. This is what makes the landscape of home—and this home—so special.

RIGHT: The curves in the pool deck are reflections of a radius that flows from inside the house out to the landscape and beyond. From the sandstone spa benches to the lap lane and ipe pool deck, the entire poolside area celebrates the views of the bay.

TOP, LEFT TO RIGHT: Grass steps carry the interior radius into the landscape. A transparent pool fence functions without interrupting the view. The pool's sandstone Lautner edge enfolds the ipe deck. ABOVE, LEFT TO RIGHT: A solid stone slab unexpectedly bridges the required drainage swale. There is little dreamier than a pool's reflections. The grass steps connect the upper lawn to the bay.

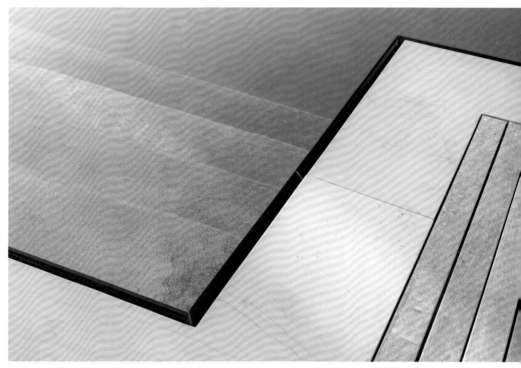

OCEAN'S EDGE

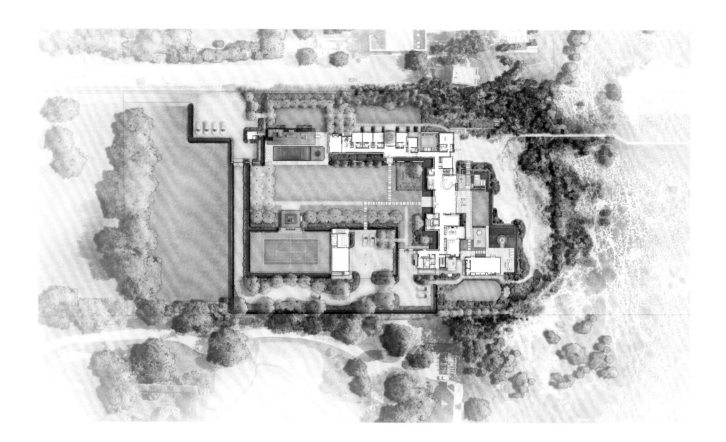

Sometimes the landscape of home emerges through a lens of long familiarity, with its keen understanding of nuance and sharp detail. This property came out of a collaboration that has roots stretching back twenty years.

We've known this diverse family, avid hosts of large groups of people, for two decades. We've worked with Leroy Street Studio, the architects, just as long. We've been friendly with Andrea Baranovich, the interior designer, and her family for decades. We've also been familiar with this site for that same amount of time. These rich relationships allowed for a depth of collaboration that resulted in an incredibly detailed marriage of architecture, land, and water.

The house is simple, clean, and incredibly elegant, and our goal here was to echo this architectural aesthetic. We edited out all the usual traditional elements of seaside homes and replaced them with a landscape designed to entice people outside. There's a pool house, pool, lounge, hot tub, and tennis/pickleball court. Covered and uncovered environments immediately adjacent to one other—the house, screened porch, veranda, landscape, lawn area, beach—invite gatherings of various sizes.

Inevitably, water defines any oceanfront property. Here, we've taken this fact to another level and integrated numerous different water features into the architecture: reflecting pools, rills, swimming pools,

PRECEDING SPREAD: With Jerusalem stone pathways, the materiality of the entry ties the landscape into the architecture. The walk to the front door traverses a bridge across a perimeter channel of water. ABOVE: Water, art, and entertaining were this landscape's driving forces. OPPOSITE TOP: The guest house walkway extends to a bosque of silver linden trees framing a gathering space. OPPOSITE: The guest house has its own pool.

LEFT: The terminus of the water feature surrounding the house is this covered area where the man-made joins nature. OVERLEAF: The overhanging pool with its built-in firepit practically becomes another living room, one that seemingly extends into the ocean. Its cantilevered structure reflects the cantilevered planes of the architecture and the landscape. No enclosure was necessary given the pool's elevation.

ABOVE, OPPOSITE: Getting the pitch of the firepit's interior slats just right for sitting comfort and eye-level perspective on the horizon required extensive experimentation and collaboration with the interior designer. The coping stone and cladding around the firepit are one and the same for visual consistency. The pool's darker areas near the deck are a sun shelf for lounging.

water walls, and fountains enhance the experience of this home from every perspective. Indeed, with water all around it, the house seems to float.

The orchestration of the indoor and outdoor spaces ensures that they flow together seamlessly. A long path leads past lawn panels and a border of maritime gardens before proceeding over a reflecting pool and into the front of the house. In the approach, the house becomes a transparent invitation to view the ocean in the distance; ultimately, the arrival and the view coincide over water.

The rear terrace and pool areas step down toward the ocean, further opening the views from the interior to the exterior. Here a covered porch unfolds to an ample lounge terrace and a lounging pool, which flows into a wraparound pool that cantilevers into space. This arrangement obviates the need for a fence, connects the landscape to the ocean beyond, and renders the music of water cascading over the infinity edge to the trough four feet below. Just off the screened porch, we designed a firepit to nest within the pool. When people sit here, they feel as if they are underwater, yet they're still eye level with horizon. A hot tub set into its own beachfront milieu is wonderfully private.

In the way this property brings together all the elements—air, water, fire, and earth—it truly celebrates life.

RIGHT: The cantilevered planes of the architecture allowed for the most astonishing landscape expression of the home as a kind of floating island unto itself yet connected to its surroundings. Here it's clear that there's water, water everywhere—and a sandy rooftop beach, floating lawn for entertaining, private spa deck for lounging tucked down and away from the home's public areas, and so much more.

TOP, LEFT TO RIGHT: The entry gates introduce the architectural palette. The tree centers an interior axis. The guest pool is steps from the interior. The main house pool overlooks the horizon. ABOVE, LEFT TO RIGHT: The house seems to float on entry. Native and naturally adapted plantings frame a private beach. Cascading water creates a joyful sound. A raised boardwalk connects the house to the beach.

HOME IN THE CITY

Being a landscape architect in the city is, as elsewhere, a bit like being a surrogate of Mother Nature, as well as an engineer. Our task is to envision and bring into being realms of beauty, private escapes, and personal oases up onto urban rooftops and terraces where no terrain to speak of exists. Here, in these environments of brick, steel, and concrete in the sky, we must build the foundational ecology of each garden: the soils and substrates in which the plants take root, the water sources and drainage, and the structures necessary to support this growing green architecture.

These planted places of joy overhead live just beyond the walls of the home, so it's critical that they directly enhance the experience of home from both vantage points, interior and exterior. Because of their limited size and closeness to home, private landscapes in the city function more like rooms than those in other contexts and require the same considered attention to lighting as the spaces indoors. Given their inevitably tight confines, there's an overwhelming need to make every square inch count, so we heighten even more our attention to textures, colors, materials, and details. And since urban gardens generally need to flourish year-round, the evergreen plants of their architecture inevitably take center stage.

The same plants tend to want to grow on urban roofscapes and terraces, especially on the East Coast, as the species that thrive along the Atlantic coast. The two environments, as dissimilar as they seem, are both harsh and from sun to wind to drainage, place surprisingly comparable pressures on plant life. Crape myrtles love both places. So do hydrangea and roses. Lavender is another hardy stalwart that's proven its ruggedness and adaptability. While we've compiled a tried-and-true palette of plants that thrive in the harsh urban environment, we constantly test new plant varieties in the city's various microclimates. The same goes for the materials—the woods, metals, tiles, and stone—that we use to construct so much of the urban garden's hardscape.

However expansive the rooftop or terrace, we still work to create the most organic relationships possible between the interior and exterior rooms, and between the architecture and the landscape. We often balance the movable furniture that's taken in at the end of the season with built-in furnishings so that families can use and enjoy the space when a random balmy day arrives unexpectedly in the very late fall, depths of winter, or early spring, as so often happens. Then we hand the landscape off in the hope that it will continue to grow, evolve, and thrive.

OPPOSITE: Privacy is always a key consideration in designing urban gardens, and layered plantings can effectively shield these intimate oases from adjacent views. Here, a forest of river birch trees underplanted with shade-tolerant perennials including a Japanese forest grass, lady's mantle, astilbe, and white Annabelle hydrangea screens a spa garden from onlookers all around.

CITY HAVEN

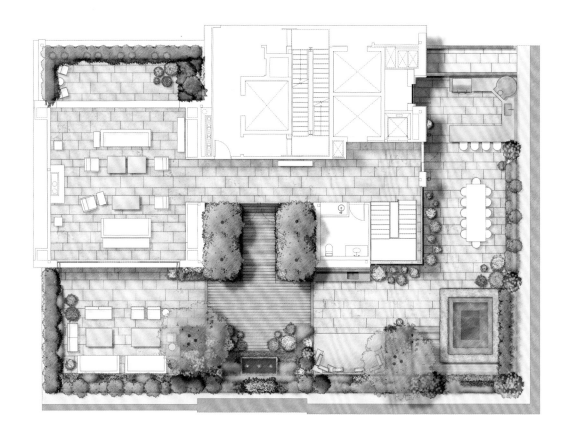

Landscaping the rooftop of a duplex in the spirit of an English garden is a fun, worthy challenge. For this expansive L-shaped terrace, and second small terrace, we collaborated with the design firm Ashe Leandro to delineate outdoor rooms off the interior rooms with sleek ipe wood planters softened by grasses and other plantings, and enclosed the entirety within a lush, vegetative border.

The entry garden opens through a cadence of crape myrtles. We reimagined the existing spa pool as an old-world treasure with a tiled interior and reclaimed granite street curbing. The media room unfolds to an exterior lounge area with a firepit and tables on one side, a bistro table and chairs on the other, and a vast sun bed for sunning and lounging nearby. Opposite, an outdoor TV integrates into a cabinet that becomes a wet focal wall when not in use. Potted culinary herbs, evergreens, and annuals add texture and more.

The result feels cohesive, detailed, and knitted together.

PRECEDING SPREAD: Set within a sea of plantings, a water feature created from a reclaimed granite trough says "welcome" at the ipe-planked terrace entry. ABOVE: In plan, the outdoor rooms unfold off their interior counterparts with consistent flooring materials for continuity. OPPOSITE: This garden is a collection of elements meant to feel carefully curated over time.

RIGHT: Borders of grasses and meadow-type perennials partition this terrace's three distinct areas—back, front, and main living/entertaining space—into smaller rooms for intimacy. These plantings, which spill out and down to the collections of terra-cotta pots sprinkled around the garden, do much to create the garden's overall aesthetic, which is natural, loose, and relaxed to such a degree that it almost looks wild. The planters, wood finishes, and furnishings take cues from the materials and forms indoors, as well as the interior fireplace wall. Instead of decorative fixtures, discreetly placed up-lighting bathes the various plantings in a soft glow that transforms the mood of the garden as the sun sets.

URBAN ESCAPE

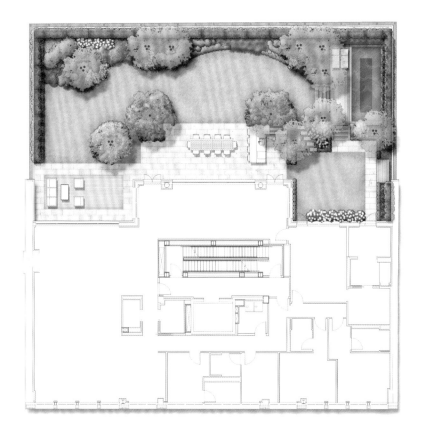

Buildings in New York City inevitably live multiple lives. They also can morph form and function from era to era. When this former parking garage was converted into a multifamily building with the addition of a new, low-rise tower, the reinvention created a substantial setback, offering these West Coast natives accustomed to an indoor-outdoor lifestyle a residence with five thousand square feet of outdoor space. We talked about the opportunities of a traditional roof-deck and using paving and planters to define and delineate the outdoor rooms. Instead, we decided to create a park with small rooms carved out for entertaining.

Right off the interior kitchen is the outdoor dining room, and directly to the left of that, off the living room, is the cocktail lounge area. We clustered all furnishings and hardscape right at the building's edge to create a seamless transition that allowed us to maximize the amount of landscape throughout. The rest of that expanse is open lawn, really a play space for the kids. This area includes a raised deck zone with a substantial soaking pool that the family can use as a play pool for the kids during the day and then convert for entertaining at night. For quieter moments, a little private garden unfolds just off the primary suite along one side of the apartment.

PRECEDING SPREAD: A grove of river birches helps transform this city terrace into an elevated park. Little Lime hydrangea, Japanese forest grasses, and hellebores thrive in its shadier components. Creeping thyme between the stepping stones releases fragrance when people brush by. OPPOSITE: Boxwood balls, a unifying motif, add winter interest. ABOVE: The berms that create soil depth for the trees establish the garden's geometry of arcs and lines.

A continuous back wall of a faux vegetation serves as a buffer from the immediate, less desirable views. In front of that, river birch trees, viburnums, and various larger shrubs provide layering and additional screening effects. Islands of plantings, punctuated by Kwanzan flowering cherry trees, a client favorite, sit in the foreground of the lounge and create a forced perspective. At ground level, a combination of pretty, sun-loving, heat- and drought-tolerant Pancium and Pennisetum grasses (with pockets of echinacea) and evergreen boxwoods live in the foreground. Toward the back, a shade perennial mix includes astilbe, hellebores, Hakone grass, Russian sage, and a clumping, noninvasive bamboo that offers an evergreen element with some movement, like grasses that sway in the wind. For the paving hardscape, we used porcelain pavers that complement the light stucco finish on the new building portion beyond.

Lighting plays an important role here because this family tends to enjoy their terraces more often at night. Up lights on the birch trees reveal the exfoliating bark, and small copper and brass path lights throughout add sparkle and glimmer, just right for the city that never sleeps.

RIGHT: A screen of faux ivy provides complete privacy along the garden's back edge; a scrim of bamboo Phyllostachys softens the effect with living plant material. The level changes that define the spa garden are functional as well as aesthetic: they conceal the structure that supports the spa's weight.

SURREY PARK

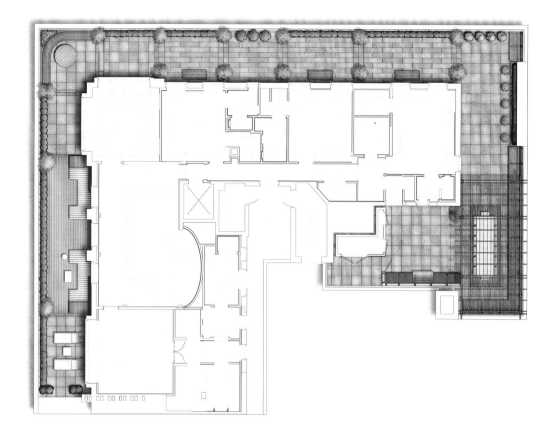

Ensuring that the landscape of an urban home melds with the interior living spaces calls for close collaboration—here with John B. Murray Architect and Cullman & Kravis. This family entertains frequently, so strategically zoning their G-shaped terrace for different activities made perfect sense. The rooftop of a favorite hotel, the Surrey on Manhattan's Upper East Side, provided many cues, including the use of wood planters that will mute over time.

We developed an area with built-in banquettes and retractable awnings with Cullman & Kravis and paved it in a warm French limestone with gradations that resemble wood. A cool gray bluestone paves the remainder of the exterior space, with ipe decking under the outdoor dining area. Plantings march in ordered rhythm down the long gallery side, punctuated for porosity. Low boxwood hedges hide the base of the guardrails and the windows of the adjacent buildings without blocking the views.

Carefully positioned fixtures in the planters' toe kicks cast a reflected glow, without causing glare when viewed from the interior rooms set below the terrace. Lights embedded in drifts of Russian sage serve as beacons. Sconces and traditional lights on the building side offer functional illumination. Pendants, sconces, and downlights layer radiance within the dining pergola next to the outdoor kitchen.

This roofscape was an exercise in doing the most with the least. To maximize the living space, we pared back the plantings. In the transition zones, they bloom.

PRECEDING SPREAD: As the cedar elements weather, they will gain a soft patina. A shallow bed behind the banquette maximizes planting space. Clipped boxwoods in low planters hide the parapet. Russian sage in elevated planters brings color, cadence, and rhythm. ABOVE: Every zone, public and private, prioritizes city views. OPPOSITE, TOP: Planter lighting provides soft, functional pathway illumination, while also breaking the reflective nature of the windows from the interior. OPPOSITE: A louvered privacy screen grounds the dining pergola to the terrace.

RIGHT: Various types of fixtures built into the pergola and the louvered wall, as well as the pair of pendants selected by Cullman & Kravis, offer ample flexibility for creating different moods and styles of illumination magic throughout the day and into the night. At the corner, round zinc pots inject a material contrast to all the wood; their tall grasses also add a wonderful element of motion when they sway with the wind. The detailing of these outdoor spaces takes many cues from the choices John B. Murray Architect made inside.

LIBERTY VIEW

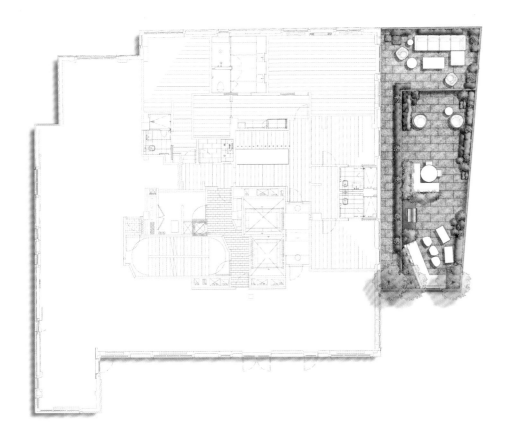

City dwellers often ask for gardens with clean, simple palettes of clipped evergreens and spare flowers. But this family requested that we take inspiration from English country gardens for their pied-à-terre, a duplex with terraces on both levels. To create that English layered effect but with minimal amounts of planting—and to maximize function—we collaborated closely with Heather Wells, their interior designer. Building off the existing paving with hand-thrown pots and custom aluminum banquettes and planters finished to resemble a living zinc patina, we tied interior and exterior spaces together with the color and materials palette.

The lounge area off the library, dining area with the outdoor kitchen tucked right behind, and social lounge on the lower level make the most of the Statue of Liberty views. Low planters tucked in between the window and the furnishings create garden views inside and out and, with the evergreens and grasses along the railing, suggest the desired layering. A scrim of fernleaf Japanese maples here will eventually grow into an overarching canopy. The lounge's florae coordinate with the interior's strong palette of oranges, bronzes, maroons, and purples in front of a background of lime hydrangea. By the kitchen, an herb garden comes in handy for making cocktails.

The couple's private oasis upstairs flourishes under the cover of the building's existing roof structure, with vegetation that frames spectacular harbor views.

PRECEDING SPREAD: Handmade clay pots and zinc-finished planters with sedum Autumn Joy and Japanese forest grass echo the interior's organic aesthetic. ABOVE: The lower terrace hosts the public areas. OPPOSITE, TOP: Hydrangea, boxwood, and taller grasses enhance the lower terrace's textural identity; culinary herbs add ornament and function. OPPOSITE: A boxwood hedge screens the upper terrace. The plantings remain consistent throughout.

VERDE MODERN

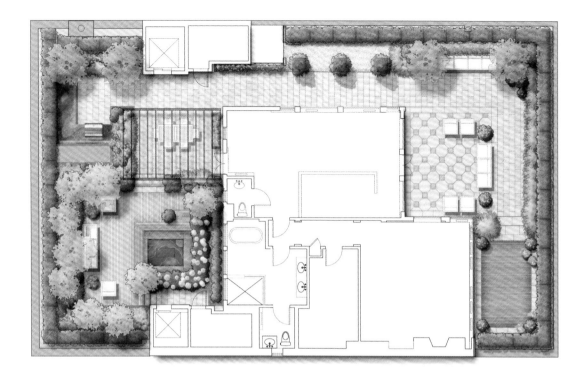

Sometimes, as with this garden oasis in midtown Manhattan, great challenges prove to be the catalyst for wonderful design. Purchased for its extensive rooftop space and breathtaking views of the Empire State Building, this prewar upper-floor apartment also came with significant limitations, structural and otherwise. Screening the entire rooftop from the view of curious neighbors was obviously key. So was organizing the available square footage into public and private zones that flowed with the interiors designed by Gary McBournie. As it turned out, the extensive structural steel work needed to support the roofscape's elements inspired the level changes that give this complex of open terraces and secluded green rooms its cohesive character.

Up several stairs, the expansive entertaining terrace makes the most of the view of the Empire State Building. The private garden, an urban Eden with an elevated spa and sitting area, opens off the primary suite; this space is protected and hidden from the entertaining areas by an outdoor catering kitchen. A pergola with a dining table offers a bower, of sorts, for more intimate meals that can also serve as a staging area for larger-scale entertaining. Last, but not least, another raised terrace is dedicated to yoga and fitness.

The roofscape's hard materials feel slightly atypical in the city, but there is a high level of refinement in the details. All the walls and terrace floors are wrapped in planks of oiled ipe wood. The spa is

PRECEDING SPREAD: Ipe planking and Indian sandstone establish the garden's aesthetic of elegant understatement. From shade to sun, boxwood, lady's mantle, and Japanese forest grass transition to hellebore, astilbe, and Annabelle hydrangea. The level changes also conceal the spa's supporting elements. OPPOSITE: Built elements combine with carefully considered plant heights to frame spectacular vistas. ABOVE: The plan prioritizes the skyline views.

finished with hand-polished copper plate that will develop a verdigris patina over time. Exposed fasteners on the pergola harken back to the neighborhood's industrial past.

A grove of birches, underplanted with astilbe and lady's mantle, envelopes and screens the private area. Banks of hydrangea cozy up to the spa, and clematis climbs the pergola, almost as if it were in the Hamptons. These layers of lush green textural components offer very soft pops of white flowers that come and go from time to time. On the other side of the terrace, we used similar materials in slightly different ways. And because we didn't want any of the plantings to feel too rigid, clipped, or laser-lined, we shaped the boxwoods that march around the perimeter into individuals as distinctive as these clients.

OPPOSITE: The more private side of the terrace centers on the spa, which opens directly off the primary bath and offers access to the nearby primary bedroom. ABOVE: Tucked away behind a planter beyond the pergola, the outdoor kitchen is not a focal point, yet it's still convenient for everyday use or by caterers and staff when the family entertains.

TOP, LEFT TO RIGHT: Instead of a continuous hedge, clipped boxwood soldiers march along one perimeter. Grasses add movement in front of the evergreens. Natchez crape myrtles combine with an arborvitae hedge to block neighboring views. ABOVE, LEFT TO RIGHT: A lounge area sits next to the spa. Japanese forest grass layers textural interest with the river birch's exfoliating bark.

My Home

More than just the family house, home is the community where we live. For my family, that is Sag Harbor on Long Island's East End. Originally the realm of Native Americans and settled by Europeans in 1730, Sag Harbor, the site of the first US Customs House and once a thriving whaling village, remains an enduring haven for artists, writers, and drinkers.

Our family house has been a gathering place for more than thirty years. When we welcomed our daughter, Renata, we put in a swimming pool by swapping one neighbor a new roof for the land and adding gates so both of our neighbors, and their friends, could use it. Comparative newcomers, we've felt embraced from the start. That's why we so wanted to put our skills and resources to work for the village.

Oakland Cemetery, which dates to 1840, was among our first community projects. When we got involved, its giant oak trees were falling, smashing old gravestones and obliterating the history these monuments represent. With the Sag Harbor Partnership, we convinced the powers that be to let us help. Local tree and landscape crews, corralled for our preservation initiative, happily offered to volunteer their time and labor—fueled by village-supplied coffee and doughnuts to prune and haul the brush.

We repeated these efforts at St. David African Methodist Episcopal Zion Cemetery, founded in 1857 as the resting place for Sag Harbor's Native American, African American, and European communities. Contributing here was a privilege. Soon after, then-mayor Sandra Schroeder asked for our help with Long Wharf. An international seaport since 1770 and rebuilt for whaling vessels in 1821, Long Wharf housed a torpedo plant during World War II. It was now crumbling. The village elders wanted to maintain its functionality and make it a community draw, but residents were concerned about parking. Our design preserved all but four parking spaces; added a forty-foot-deep public area for congregating; created a perimeter pedestrian boardwalk that, in time, will connect to the recently opened John Steinbeck Waterfront Park; and improved the marine environment by collecting, trapping, and filtering the runoff that previously emptied directly into the bay.

When April Gornik and Eric Fischl transformed an abandoned Methodist church into an artists' center,

OPPOSITE TOP: In Sag Harbor, front gardens like mine are part of the public streetscape as well as a welcome home. OPPOSITE: The backyard is our family sanctuary. The screened porch and pool terrace flow together to invite indoor-outdoor living. The river birch trees framing the yard provide shade during the day and captivating light in the evening.

we worked with architect Lee Skolnick to shape the landscape for gatherings. We also developed a master plan for Mashashimuet Park on land donated by Margaret Olivia Slocum Sage, the force behind many of the community's public amenities.

John Steinbeck Waterfront Park, the first park built in Sag Harbor in more than a century, has been our most rewarding project to date. Over four mayoral administrations, with a coalition of local interests, we developed a design that celebrates the waterfront. This park epitomizes a recycle, reuse, and replant approach, incorporating leftover construction materials and also trees, shrubs, stonework, sand for new dunes, native plants, and rain gardens donated by local nurseries and contractors.

The most personal of all our endeavors is Jean's Walk, a public pathway shaded by crape myrtles that we created in remembrance of my mother, which leads to Cilli Farm. Our efforts in Sag Harbor are ongoing. These projects, done gratis, are immensely gratifying because they contribute to the lives of many people, some of whom we'll never know. It's an honor when the village calls. For us, it's the landscape of home.

ABOVE: A preliminary rendering for John Steinbeck Waterfront Park highlights the focus on its location. OPPOSITE TOP: Long Wharf's new esplanade, which will eventually connect to John Steinbeck Waterfront Park beyond the windmill, beckons strollers to experience the entirety of this icon of Sag Harbor history. OPPOSITE: Long Wharf's newly created public gathering space allows visitors immediate access to the harbor.

TOP, LEFT TO RIGHT: The sign for the opening of John Steinbeck Waterfront Park; the view across the park's dune scape; the park's amphitheater; amphitheater seating of native Montauk boulder slices. ABOVE, LEFT TO RIGHT: Crape myrtles along Jean's Walk, planted in my mother's honor; tree work in Oakland Cemetery; the old Methodist church, now an artists' haven; areas created there for entertaining and gathering.

ACKNOWLEDGMENTS

We could not do what we do without collaborating with some of the world's greatest architects and designers. The landscape of home is as much about their work as ours, for it is the combination and integration of interior and exterior spaces that make home such a special place.

We give great thanks to those who bring our projects to fruition:

To the nurserymen who grow the trees and plants.

To the landscapers who place and dig and plant the trees, shrubs, flowers, and grasses.

To the boys on the bulldozers and excavators who skillfully grade and sculpt the land.

To the masons who build the walls and terraces.

To the pool specialists who make water do magical things.

To the lighting professionals who create enchantment in the garden.

To those who build our golf greens and tennis, pickleball, and paddle courts that make home more fun for all.

And finally, to the maintenance experts who care for the gardens, lawns, trees, orchards, vegetable gardens, and meadows, making them a healthy place both for our clients as well as the birds, bees, and butterflies that also call our landscapes home.

We are so fortunate to lead a hardworking, talented team of professionals who make extraordinary things possible. With appreciation and gratitude to all those who make up Hollander Design today:

Jing Bian
Joseph Blau
Hope Brice
Bailey Briggs
Alexandria Chomyn
Maryanne Connelly
Richard Conte
Jose Correa
Lily D'Ambrosio
William Dinan
Caitlin Drury
Restituto Dumalos
Stephen Eich
Griffin Felski
Jeana Pearl Fletcher
Stuart Harriott
Liza Killian
Nicholas Lee

Michelle Lin-Luse
Anna McKeigue
Robert Jeff McLeod
Fareed Mohammed
Ryan Morrison
Kerri Murphy
Daniel Perenyi
Suko Presseau
Melissa Reavis
Jim Romanshek
Tucker Schnaars
Alexis Stanhope
Alison Strickler
Rebecca Tran
Ritchie Tumulak
Geoffrey Valentino
Justin Willard
J. Howard Williams

Special thanks to the exceptional team responsible for creating this beautiful book: Charles Miers, Kathleen Jayes, Doug Turshen, Judith Nasatir, Steve Turner, and photographers Charles Mayer, Neil Landino, and Joshua McHugh.

First published in the United States of America in 2024 by
Rizzoli International Publications, Inc.
300 Park Avenue South
New York, NY 10010
www.rizzoliusa.com

Copyright © 2024 Edmund D. Hollander Landscape Architect
Design, P. C.
Text: Judith Nasatir
Foreword: Bunny Williams
Site plans: Hollander Design

Photography Credits:
Charles Mayer: pages 14, 16-17, 20-21, 22-23, 26, 27, 30
(bottom right), 31 (bottom left), 34, 36, 37, 38-39,
40 (top right), 42-43, 45, 48-49, 50-51 (top and bottom left,
top right), 52-53, 55, 56-57, 58-59, 60-61, 63, 64-65,
66-67, 68-69, 76-77, 92, 93, 99, 106 (bottom center), 118-119,
120-121, 126-127, 132, 134-135, 137, 138, 139, 140, 141, 142-143,
144-145, 156, 157, 160-161, 163, 164-165, 166-167, 216, 218-19,
221, 222-23, 230-231, 233, 234-235, 240-241, 242, 244,
245, 246-247, 249, 251, 252 (bottom left and right)

Hollander Design: pages 11, 31 (top left), 50-51 (bottom
center), 73 (bottom), 86, 116-117 (bottom left and center),
102-103, 250

Joshua McHugh: 32-33, 224-225, 226, 228-229,
236-237, 239

Neil Landino: 2-3, 5, 6, 8, 13, 19, 24-25, 28-29, 30 (top and
bottom left, top right), 31 (top and bottom right), 40 (top and
bottom left, bottom right), 41, 46, 47, 50-51 (top center, bottom
right), 70-71, 73 (top), 74-75, 78-79, 80-81, 83, 84-85, 87,
88-89, 90-91, 94, 95, 96-97, 100-101, 104-105, 106 (top and
bottom left, center top, and top and bottom right), 107 (top and
bottom), 108-109, 111, 112-113, 114-115, 116-117 (top left, center,
and right, bottom right), 123, 124, 125, 128, 129, 130-131,
146-147, 149, 150-151, 152-153, 154-155, 158-159, 168-169,
171, 172-173, 174-175, 176-177, 178-179, 180, 181, 182-183,
185, 186-187, 188-189, 190-191, 192-193, 194-195, 197,
198-199, 200-201, 202-203, 205, 206-207, 208-209,
210, 211, 212-213, 214-215, 252 (top left and right), 253, 255

Publisher: Charles Miers
Senior Editor: Kathleen Jayes
Design: Doug Turshen with Steve Turner
Production Manager: Colin Hough Trapp
Managing Editor: Lynn Scrabis

Printed in China

2024 2025 2026 2027 / 10 9 8 7 6 5 4 3 2

ISBN: 978-0-8478-9977-7

Library of Congress Control Number: 2023919590

Visit us online:
Facebook.com/RizzoliNewYork
Twitter: @Rizzoli_Books
Instagram.com/RizzoliBooks
Pinterest.com/RizzoliBooks
Youtube.com/user/RizzoliNY
Issuu.com/Rizzoli